GRADING TERMS

A "good" coin is so worn that most of the detail has disappeared. These are not featured: only very rare specimens have any value.

FINE	A coin worn by considerable use, but still retaining clear lettering and some of the finer detail (hair, for example, not just a 'parting').
V.F.	The highest parts of a VERY FINE coin will show signs of its having been circulated. It must, however, possess a pleasing appearance devoid of disfiguring marks.
E.F.	An EXTREMELY FINE coin is almost perfect; close examination revealing traces of wear to the highest parts.
Unc.	UNCIRCULATED - unworn, as struck by the mint.
PROOF	is not a measure of condition, but a description of the method of manufacture. Certain exceptions apart; the field ("unprinted" part) will possess a mirror-like polish; the inscription, legend, or other design, will have a "frosted" appearance; the whole having an effect of great beauty which the smallest scratch will impair.

Excepting rare coins, the value of which is determined by the fact that nothing better is available, to be "collectable" a coin should possess (at least) the requirements of FINE given above. The 'head' should not be worn to a silhouette. The grading should never be qualified by "for its age": a FINE coin of 1800 should be no more worn than a FINE one of 1900 despite the hundred years age difference. The presence of ALL THE ORIGINAL DETAIL but with the highest parts barely flattened (new but 'shop-soiled') would be considered EXTREMELY FINE. Even uncirculated specimens will vie for honours according to freedom from mint bag-marks, brilliance etc., until the rare title of F.D.C. (fleur de coin) is awarded.

MARKETING

It is generally accepted that for the majority of coins a dealer's buying price is about 50% of his/her selling price. The dealer, in effect, is out-of-pocket until a buyer is found. A different 'deal' can be made where the coin is much sought after, particularly if the dealer has a customer in mind. Auction houses attract groups of buyers: collectors and dealers. Advertising, as you would to sell any other commodity, should stress any variety e.g. Obv.3 + Rev.B rather than a bare coin-date-condition. See, also, footnotes on pages 15 and 16.

CLEANING and POLISHING

A dealer's or auctioneer's list will sometimes indicate that a coin has been cleaned; a lower price results: the lesson should be clear. Cleaning diminishes value; polishing will TOTALLY DESTROY.

V.A.T. REGULATIONS: all coins less than 100 years old, whether or not they are legal tender, when supplied by VAT registered persons, are taxable at the present Standard Rate.

GW00371692

ARD BOOK No: 0-948964-24-3
with each edition)
ARD SERIAL NUMBER: 0262-9712
nging as the title)

ORS' COINS"

on © 1997

...g order of face-value

QUARTER-FARTHINGS to CROWNS
DECIMAL CENT to FIVE POUNDS

Copper, Bronze, Silver, Nickel-brass and Cupro-nickel

EVERY non-gold coin from 1820 separately listed for:

GEORGE III	See page 48	1760 - 1820
GEORGE IV	House of HANOVER	1820 - 1830
WILLIAM IV	House of HANOVER	1830 - 1837
VICTORIA	House of HANOVER	1837 - 1901
EDWARD VII	SAXE-COBURG	1901 - 1910
GEORGE V	House of WINDSOR	1910 - 1936
EDWARD VIII	House of WINDSOR	1936
GEORGE VI	House of WINDSOR	1936 - 1952
ELIZABETH II	House of WINDSOR	1952 to date

ONE HUNDRED and SEVENTYFIVE YEARS

Photographs of coins, and information extracted from its reports, are reproduced with the permission of the Royal Mint.

A compilation of averaged selling-prices drawn from dealers' lists, auctions and numismatic magazines by

R. J. Marles for:

ROTOGRAPHIC PUBLICATIONS · 37 St. Efrides Road
Torquay · TQ2 5SG · U.K.

QUARTER FARTHINGS FOR USE IN CEYLON

Date	Mintage	Fine	V.F.	E.F.	abt Unc/FDC
VICTORIA	YOUNG HEAD				COPPER
1839	3,840,000	£9	£15	£33	£50/£75
1851	included below	£9	£15	£35	£60/£95
1852	2,215,000	£8	£12	£25	£40/£65
1853	included above	£9	£15	£30	£55/£80
1853	Proofs	(from the sets)		---	£200
1853	Cupro-nickel proofs		(P1615)	---	£225/£260
1868	Bronze proofs		(P1616)	---	£200

THIRD FARTHINGS FOR USE IN MALTA

Date	Mintage	Fine	V.F.	E.F.	abt Unc/FDC
GEORGE IV					COPPER
1827		£4	£8	£15	£40/£60
1827	Proof	---	--	£45	£175/£200
WILLIAM IV					COPPER
1835		£4	£8	£15	£40/£60
1835	noted (Seaby 1990)	GEF much lustre £25			---/---
1835	Proof	---	---	£160	---/---
VICTORIA	YOUNG HEAD				
1844	1,301,040 COPPER	£9	£15	£40	£60/£85
1844	RE (for REG)	(P1607)	---	£225	£300/£400
1844	Large 'G'	---	£18	£45	£65/£95
	"BUN" HEAD				
1866	576,000 BRONZE	£2	£5	£10	£20/£30
1868	144,000 "	£2	£5	£12	£25/£40
1876	162,000 "	£2	£5	£12	£25/£40
1878	288,000 "	£2	£5	£10	£20/£30
1881	144,000 "	£2	£5	£12	£25/£40
1884	144,000 "	£2	£3	£12	£20/£30
1885	288,000 "	£2	£4	£10	£20/£30

Proofs: 1866 £135; 1868, 1876, 1881 rarely seen.

Date	Mintage	Fine	V.F.	E.F.	abt Unc/FDC
EDWARD VII					BRONZE
1902	288,000	£2	£5	£10	£15/£25
1902	noted (Seaby 1990)	---	---	abt Unc £6	
GEORGE V					BRONZE
1913	288,000	£2	£5	£10	£15/£25

HALF FARTHINGS FOR USE IN CEYLON

Date	Mintage	Fine	V.F.	E.F.	Unc/abt. FDC.
GEORGE IV	LAUREATE HEAD				COPPER
1828	7,680,000 Rev A	£3	£7	£30	£50/£75
1828	Rev B see below	£10	£30	£75	£150/£250
1830	8,776,320	£2	£12	£30	£50/£75
1830	Smaller date	£3	£16	£50	---/----
1830	Rev B see below	£12	£40	£85	£175/----

A number of proofs occur but no transactions noted.
Rev A: trident reaches above base of letters
Rev B: the trident reaches base of letters

Date	Mintage	Fine	V.F.	E.F.	Unc/abt. FDC.
WILLIAM IV					COPPER
1837	1,935,360	£12	£35	£85	£140/£180
1837	(Seaby 1990)	---	"gdVF"	£45	---/---
VICTORIA	YOUNG HEAD				COPPER EXCEPT WHERE INDICATED
1839	2,042,880	£3	£6	£15	£40/£55
1842		£3	£5	£12	£30/£50
1843	3,440,640	£2	£4	£8	£16/£30
1844	6,451,000	£2	£4	£8	£16/£30
1844	E of REGINA over N	£3	£9	£18	£35/£60
1847	3,010,560	£3	£5	£18	£40/£65
1851	Unknown P1597	£4	£8	£20	£40/£55
1851	1 struck over 5 (noted 1995)		£16	---	£60/---
1852	989,184	---	£8	£18	£30/£45
1853	955,224	£4	£20	£25	£45/£65
1854	677,376	£9	£10	£40	£80/£140
1856	913,920 P1603	£12	£30	£50	£100/£200
1856	(noted 1995)	"Superb BU full lustre"			£250
1856	Large date	£16	£36	(not in Peck)	
1868	Bronze proof P1605	---	---	---	---/£175
1868	Cupro-nickel proof	---	---	---	---/£250

Proofs 1839 £200; 1853 £200; 1853 bronze £200

COPPER

GEORGE IV — Laureate Head — DATE BELOW BRITANNIA

Date	Mintage	Peck No.	Fine	V.F.	E.F.	abt. Unc/FDC
1821	2,688,000	P1407	£2	£6	£12	£40/£60
1821	G of GRATIA over O (Colin Cooke mint state £69)					
1821	Proof in copper		---	---	---	£350/---
1822	5,924,352	P1409	£1	£2	£15	£40/£60
1822	Proof in copper		---	---	---	£350/---
1822	Obverse 2	P1411	£1	£2	£15	£40/£60
1823	2,365,440	P1412	£2	£6	£18	£50/£75
1823	Date has I for 1		£5	£16	£30	£65/£95
1825	4,300,800 Obv.1	P1414	£2	£4	£12	£40/£60
1825	5 over 3 (Noted 1993)		£25	---	£45	---/---
1825	D of DEI over U		£10	£40	£90	---/---
1825	Obverse 2	P1414A	£4	£8	£20	£50/£75
1825	Proof in gold	P1415	---	---	extremely rare	
1826	6,666,240	P1416	£1	£3	£15	£35/£50
1826	I for 1	noted	£80	---	---	£350/---

Undraped or Bare Head — DATE BELOW HEAD

Date	Mintage	Peck No.	Fine	V.F.	E.F.	abt. Unc/FDC
1826	Inc. above	P1439	£1	£3	£12	£45/£65
1826	Roman I for 1 in date		(1993)		"Choice uncirculated"	£200
1826	Bronzed Proof	P1440	---	---	£50	£95/£125
1826	Copper Proof	P1441	---	---	£60	---/---
1827	2,365,440	P1442	£2	£4	£20	£65/£90
1828	2,365,440	P1443	£2	£3	£15	£60/£85
1829	1,505,280	P1444	£3	£9	£30	£70/£95
1830	2,365,440	P1445	£2	£4	£20	£60/£85
1830	Noted 1993		---	---	"Superb"	£95

All dies are punched more than once. If one blow fails to register with another, then figures appear doubled, even trebled: this is very common. A major misalignment, however, will add value to the coin.

Obverse 1: Peck says 'the leaf-midribs (if present) are single raised lines'
Obverse 2: The 3 lowest leaves have incuse midribs.

Patterns V Proofs - If the currency which follows differs then the pattern remains as such. If, however, the currency is based on the pattern then the pattern becomes a proof of that currency. The pattern is a "loner", the proof has "friends".

WILLIAM IV — COPPER — DATE BELOW HEAD - 21mm

Date	Mintage	Peck No.	Fine	V.F.	E.F.	abt. Unc/FDC
1831	2,688,000	P1466	£2	£5	£16	£50/£75
1831	Proof	P1467	----	bronzed		£200/£300
1831	Proof	P1468	inverted	reverse		---/£150
1831	Proof	P1469	----	copper		---/£375
1834	1,935,360 Rev.A	P1470	£2	£5	£16	£50/£75
1834	Reverse B	P1471	£2	£6	£25	£60/£95
1835	1,720,320 Rev.A	P1472	£2	£6	£30	£60/£95
1835	Reverse B	P1473	£2	£5	£16	£50/£75
1836	1,290,240	P1474	£3	£6	£25	£60/£95
1837	3,010,560	P1475	£2	£5	£20	£50/£75

Reverse B has raised line down the arms of saltire (cross of St.Andrew); whereas A has incuse line

"POINTINGS" are very much the key to some varieties. A principal feature such as a letter or ornament is selected and its 'attitude' is used to indicate the use of a different die-punch. Thus HALFPENNY indicates that the upright of the 'L' is *pointing* to a rim bead. HALFPENNY that 'L' points between two beads. Many dies are used to complete a full year's striking. New dies are usually identical being from the same, original punch. Differences are, therefore, interesting nusmismatically and unequal strikings must, eventually, show up in valuations.

FARTHINGS

VICTORIA YOUNG HEAD COPPER · DATE BELOW HEAD · 21mm

Date	Mintage	Peck No.	Fine	V.F.	E.F.	abt. Unc/FDC
1838	591,360	P1553	£2	£4	£15	£50/£75
1838	Variety DEF : on	P1553	£3	£6	£25	---/---
1839	4,300,800	P1554	£1	£3	£12	£30/£50
1839	Proofs in copper, some bronzed. Bronzed					---/£180
1839	Two pronged trident		---	£3	£12	£30/£65
1840	3,010,560	P1559	£1	£3	£12	£25/£45
1840	Variety DEF.. on	P1559	£1	£3	£12	---/---
1841	1,720,320	P1560	£1	£4	£13	£25/£45
1841	Varieties P1560	REG. and REG for REG:			£15	£30/£50
1841	Proof	P1561		If offered could fetch £800		
1842	1,290,240	P1562	£4	£9	£25	£60/£95
1842	Variety on P1562		£5	(large '42' in date)		---/---
1843	Struck over 1842		---	---	---	---/---
1843	4,085,760	P1563	£1	£3	£10	£20/£50
1843	I for 1 in date		£25	£50	£100	£200/---
1844	430,080	P1565	£25	£50	£225	£500/£650
1844	(At auction 1987)		"Mint state"		---	£836
1845	3,225,600	P1566	£1	£3	£12	£30/£60
1845	Large date		£45	"F/gdF"	(Colin Cooke 1991)	
1846	2,580,480	P1567	£5	£10	£32	£60/£85
1847	3,879,720	P1568	£1	£3	£10	£20/£50
1847	Proof		Guesstimate		---	£1500
1848	1,290,246	P1569	£1	£4	£12	£30/£65
1849	645,120	P1570	£6	£21	£50	£100/£200
1850	430,080	P1571	£1	£4	£14	£30/£60
1850	5 over inverted 5 ᘏ		---	---		---/---
	possibly, 5 over damaged 5 (no upright stroke) and much like a 3					
1850	5 over 4 Noted 1993		"gdEF"	£35	abtUNC £45	
1851	1,935,360	P1572	£6	£15	£30	£60/£95
1851	D of DEI STRUCK OVER ᑌ		£200	£500	---	---/---
1852	822,528	P1574	£5	£15	£30	£65/£120
1853	1,028,628	P1575	30p	£1	£4	£20/£30
1853	3 struck over 2		---	---	---	£45/£70
1853	Proof, bronzed, with inverted reverse			---	---	---/---
1853	Proof with raised W.W.	P1577		---		£250/£350
1853	WW incuse	P1578	£2	£6	£15	£25/£40
1853	Proof with incuse W W	P1579		---		£200/£300

VICTORIA YOUNG HEAD COPPER · DATE BELOW HEAD · 21mm

Date	Mintage	Peck No.	Fine	V.F.	E.F.	abt. Unc/FDC
1854	6,504,960	P1580	£2	£4	£10	£30/£60
1855	3,440,640	P1581 W W incuse		£9	£25	£55/£90
1855	Included	P1582 W.W. raised		£9	£25	£55/£90
1856	1,771,392	P1583		£6	£20	£45/£90
1856★	R over E (VICTORIA)	P1584	£15	£60	£100	£325/---
1856★	Noted 1992	"Fine/gdFine"	£17		Mason World Coins	
1857	1,075,200	P1585	£1	£3	£10	£20/£40
1858	1,720,320	P1586	£1	£4	£12	£25/£45
1858	Small date		£10	£20	£50	---/---
1859	1,290,240	P1587	£10	£20	£50	£75/£125
1860	Obverse date currency			C. Cooke 1990 abt Unc £3900		
1860	Obverse date proof			C. Cooke 1990 abt Unc £3600		
1864	(Cooke 1993)	P1589		Coin not selling even at £7,500!		

VICTORIA "BUN" HEAD BRONZE · DATE BELOW BRITANNIA · 20mm

BB = Border of Beads TB = Toothed Border

Date	Mintage	Peck No.	Fine	V.F.	E.F.	abt. Unc/FDC
1860	2,867,200 with various "Berries-in-Wreath" obverses:					
1860	BB 3 berries	P1854	£2	£5	£10	£20/£30
1860	Proof	P1856	---	---	---	£175
1860	MULE combining beaded and toothed borders:					
		P1857	£100	£200	£400	£1200/---
1860	TB 4 berries	P1858	50p	£2	£5	£10/£20
1860	Bronze proof		---	---	---	£200/£300
1860	TB 5 berries	P1859	50p	£2	£6	£18/£25
1860	(noted 1996)	P1859	---	"Full lustre"		£26
1861	8,601,600 4 berries	P1860	£1	£2	£8	£16/£24
1861	Bronze proof	(Cooke 1993)		"choice FDC"		---/£165
1861	Obv. 3 (5 berries)		£1	£2	£6	£12/£20
1861	Date has small '8'		£2	£4	£12	£25/---
1862	14,336,000	P1865	50p	£1.80	£4	£12/£25
1862	Proof		---	---	£200	---/---
1862	Large 8 over small 8		(1990)		£30	---/---
1863	1,433,600	P1867	£15	£30	£60	£125/£250
1864	2,508,800 serif 4	P1869	---	£6	£10	£20/£40
1864	plain 4		---	£9	£15	£30/£50
1864	COPPER see P1589	Date Below Head		See Young Head above		

★ 1856 Also described as E over R. Either R was struck over an incorrect E, or E was wrongly selected to improve a poor R. (or ?)

HARINGTON and LENNOX farthing tokens are to be found in "Collectors' Coins: Ireland" (they feature the 'Irish' harp).
From James I to Charles I there were Richmond rounds - Transitional, Maltravers rounds, Richmond ovals and Maltravers ovals.

VICTORIA (continued) DATE BELOW BRITANNIA - 20mm

Date	Mintage	Peck	Fine	V.F.	E.F.	abt. Unc/FDC
1865	4,659,200	P1873	£1	£4	£8	£15/£30
1865	5 over 2	P1872A	£1	£3	£12	£25/£60
1865	5 over 3	---	£1	£4	£14	£20/£35
1865	Date has small '8'		£2	£8	£16	£32/---
1866	3,584,000	P1875	£1	£3	£9	£18/£30
1867	5,017,600	P1878	£1	£3	£8	£18/£35
1868	4,851,208	P1881	£1	£3	£8	£18/£35
1868	Bronze proof	P1882	---	---	---	£145/£250
1869	3,225,600	P1884	£2	£6	£15	£35/£60
1872	2,150,400	P1885	£1	£3	£6	£20/£30
1873	3,225,620	P1886	£1	£2	£5	£15/£25
1873	Low set 3 in date		---	---	£8	£16/£30

Proofs also occur for 1861, 1862, 1863, 1866, 1867.

OBVERSE 4 'AGED' (MATRONLY) BUST - still 'BUN' HEAD

'H' (centred below date) = Heaton Mint

Date	Mintage	Peck	Fine	V.F.	E.F.	abt. Unc/FDC
1874H	3,584,000	P1887	45p	£2	£6	£18/£30
1874H	Bronze proof	(noted 1991)		"about FDC"		---/£170
1874H	Gs struck over ⅁s		£50	£120	£240	£425/£600
1875	712,760	P1890	£5	£10	£22	£60/£85
1875	Large date	(5 berries)	£5	£12	£25	£65/£90
1875	Small date	(5 berries)	£6	£22	£45	£100/£300
1875	Small date	(4 berries)	£5	£25	£50	£175/£350
1875H	6,092,800	P1892	25p	75p	£5	£20/£30
1876H	1,175,200	P1894	£4	£9	£25	£60/£100
1876	RF.G for REG		£5	---	---	---/---
1877	Proofs only	P1895	bronze	(Cooke '93)		£2350
1877	Bronzed proof		guesstimate			£1400/£1600
1878	4,008,540	P1896	25p	75p	£5	£15/£30
1878	Proof	P1897	---	---	---	--/£325
1879	3,977,180	P1898	25p	75p	£5	£15/£30
1879	Date has large '9'		£1	£4	£8	£20/£40
1880	1,842,710 4 berries	P1899	£1	£3	£9	£25/£35
1880	3 berries	P1901	£2	£20	£40	£60/£100
1881	See below Obv.4	P1901A	£20	£30	£40	£80/£120
1881	3,494,670 Obv.5	P1902	50p	£2	£4	£15/£30
1881H	1,792,000	P1904	£1	£3	£6	£12/£22
1882H	1,792,000	P1905	75p	£2	£7	£14/---
1883	1,128,680	P1907	£2	£4	£16	£30/£50
1884	5,782,000	P1909	15p	50p	£1	£10/£25
1885	5,442,308	P1911	25p	£1	£2	£10/£25
1886	7,767,790	P1913	25p	£1	£2	£9/£20
1887	1,340,800	P1915	£1	£2	£7	£16/£30
1888	1,887,250	P1916	75p	£1	£5	£12/£25
1890	2,133,070	P1917	75p	£1	£5	£12/£25

Proofs, in bronze, for all except 1876H and 1879.

VICTORIA continued - mainly obverse 5 - BRONZE

Date	Mintage	Peck	Fine	V.F.	E.F.	abt. Unc/FDC
1891	4,959,690	P1919	50p	£2	£5	£12/£20
1892	887,240	P1921	£5	£10	£20	£45/£65
1893	3,904,320	P1923	£1	£2	£6	£12/£25
1893	Narrower date		£2	£4	£12	£25/£50
1894	2,396,770	P1924	£2	£4	£12	£20/£30
1895	2,852,852	P1925	£6	£12	£25	£60/£90

Proofs occur except 1881H, 1887, 1888,1893, 1895.

'Old' or 'Widow' Head

Date	Mintage	Peck	Fine	V.F.	E.F.	abt. Unc/FDC
1895	Inc above	P1958	50p	£2	£6	£12/£18
1896	3,668,610	P1959	50p	£2	£6	£12/£18
1896	(noted 1996)	"Full lustre, quite exceptional"				£18
1897	4,579,800:	blackened to distinguish from half-sovereign				
1897	Undarkened	P1961	£1	£3	£10	£20/£35
1897 *	Horizon as P1961 but black finish			---	---	£12/£18
1897 **	Higher horizon	P1962	50p	£2	£6	£12/£18
1898	4,010,080	P1963	50p	£2	£6	£12/£18
1899	3,864,616	P1964	50p	£2	£6	£12/£18
1900	5,969,317	P1965	50p	£2	£6	£12/£18
1901	8,016,459	P1966	50p	£1	£4	£8/£12

Proofs occur for 1896 and, possibly, for 1901

Obverse 4 has 4 berries in wreath arranged as two pairs (2+2 and not 1+2+1 as previously). Obverse 5 has 3 berries arranged 2+1.

* Rev A 7 points *TO* a border tooth

** Rev B 7 points *BETWEEN* two teeth

EDWARD VII BRONZE · 20mm

Date	Mintage	Fine	V.F.	E.F.	Unc/FDC
1902	5,125,120	25p	£1	£4	£8/£12
1903	5,331,200 low horizon	30p	£2	£5	£10/£18
1904	3,628,800	75p	£3	£6	£12/£18
1905	4,076,800	25p	£2	£6	£12/£20
1906	5,340,160	25p	£2	£6	£12/£20
1907	4,399,360	25p	£2	£6	£12/£20
1908	4,264,960	20p	£1	£5	£10/£15
1909	8,852,480	20p	£1	£4	£9/£14
1910	2,598,400	£1.50	£3	£6	£14/£21

All chemically darkened to avoid confusion with gold.

FARTHINGS BRONZE · 20mm

GEORGE V

ALL DARKENED, CHEMICALLY, UNTIL 1918

Date	Mintage		Fine	V.F.	E.F.	abt. Unc./FDC
1911	5,196,800	(see foot of page)	25p	£1	£4	£6/£12
1912	7,669,760			40p	£1.50	£5/£7
1913	4,184,320			65p	£1.50	£5/£7
1914	6,126,988	BRITT obv 1		65p	£3	£9/£14
1914		BRIT T obv 2		65p	£3	£9/£14
1915		BRITT		£40	"Guesstimate"	---/---
1915	7,129,254	BRIT T		65p	£4	£12/£16
1915	Noted 1993			---	"Superb"	£16
1916	10,993,325			25p	£1	£3/£6
1917	21,434,844			15p	£1	£3/£4
1918	19,362,818 left bright			15p	£1	£2/£3
1918	Rare darkened finish			---	£6	£10/£15
1919	15,089,425			20p	£1	£3/£6
1920	11,480,536			20p	£1	£3/£6
1921	9,469,097			20p	£1	£2/£5
1922	9,956,983			20p	£1	£4/£8
1923	8,034,457			25p	£1	£5/£10
1924	8,733,414			25p	£1	£4/£6
1925	12,634,697			20p	£1	£4/£6
1926	9,792,397			20p	75p	£4/£6
1927	7,868,355			15p	50p	£3/£5
1928	11,625,600			15p	75p	£2/£4
1929	8,419,200			15p	75p	£2/£4
1930	4,195,200			15p	£1	£3/£5
1931	6,595,200			15p	£1	£3/£5
1931	Bronze proof	(Peck 2347)		---	---	/£165
1932	9,292,800			15p	50p	£3/£5
1932	Bronze proof	Noted 1993		"A super FDC"		/£163
1933	4,560,000			20p	£1	£4/£6
1933	Proof	(Peck 2353) (1993)		---	---	£195
1934	3,052,800			25p	£1.50	£5/£8
1934	Proof	(Peck 2355) (1993)		"Stunning FDC"		£195
1935	2,227,200			65p	£3	£12/£18
1936	9,734,400	★ issued posthumously		15p	25p	£1/£2.50

'Fine' are sold, usually from 'The Tray' 5p to 25p

1911 The 'standard' Peck obverse 1 has two variations:
Obverse 1a = above B.M. the neck is hollow.
Obverse 1b = above B.M. the neck is flat.
At present, values are identical even amongst dealers who DO distinguish the variety - many don't; but more are doing so.

EDWARD VIII Duke of Windsor

1937 Extremely rare - not issued for general circulation.

GEORGE VI

Date	Details		Peck No.	V.F.	E.F.	abt. Unc/FDC/FDC
1937	8,131,200		---	---	40p	---/ £1/ £2
1937	26,402	proofs	---	---	---	£3/ £4/ £6
1938	7,449,600		---	20p	50p	£3/ £6/ £9
1939	31,440,000		---	---	15p	45p/90p/ £1
1940	18,360,000		---	---	25p	80p/ £1/ £2
1941	27,312,000		---	---	20p	60p/80p/ £1
1942	28,857,600		---	---	20p	60p/80p/ £1
1943	33,345,600		---	---	20p	60p/80p/ £1
1944	25,137,600		---	---	15p	40p/60p/75p
1945	23,736,000		---	---	15p	40p/60p/75p
1946	23,364,800		---	---	15p	60p/80p/ £1
1946	Bronze proof (1991)		P2476	(possibly 3 only)		£225
1947	14,745,600		---	---	15p	60p/80p/ £1
1948	16,622,400		---	---	15p	60p/80p/ £1
1949	8,424,000		---	---	20p	75p/ £2/ £3
1949	Bronze proof (1994) "One of possibly 3 or 4"					£225
1950	10,324,800		---	---	15p	40p/60p/75p
1950	17,513	proofs	---	---	---	£3/ £5/ £7
1951	14,016,000		---	---	---	40p/60p/75p
1951	20,000	proofs	---	---	---	£4/ £5/ £6
1952	5,251,200		---	---	15p	60p/80p/ £1
1952	Bronze proof		P2488	---	---	£125/£175/---
1952	Bronze proof Noted 1993 "Choice FDC, excessively rare"					£225

ELIZABETH II

Date	Details		Peck No.	V.F.	E.F.	abt. Unc/FDC/FDC
1953	6,131,037 :					
1953	Obv.1	Rev. A	P2520	Currency Set		50p/ £1/£1.50
1953	Obv.1	Rev. B	P2520A	---	---	£10/£20/---
1953	Obv.2	Rev. A	P2520B	---	---	£15/£25/£35
1953	Obv.2	Rev. B	P2521	---	10p	40p/75p/ £1
1953	40,000 proofs		P2522 (of P2521)		---	£2/ £4/ £6
1953	Proofs	2 + A				£40/£60/£80
1954	6,566,400		---	---	15p	25p/35p/80p
1955	5,779,200		---	---	20p	30p/60p/90p
1956	1,996,800		---	---	30p	50p/75p/ £1

Obverse 1 is poorly defined · the cross points TO a border bead.
Obverse 2 is sharper · the cross points BETWEEN two border beads.
Reverse A (dies of George VI) · 'F' points BETWEEN two beads.
Reverse B is similar but the 'F' points TO a border bead.

1953 Obverse/Reverse Rarity Scale 1 + A (C) 2 + A (R)
1 + B (R) 2 + B (VC)
(R) = Rare · (C) = Common · (VC) = Very Common

GEORGE IV — LAUREATE HEAD — COPPER 28mm

Date	Mintage		Fine	V.F.	E.F.	abt. Unc/FDC.
1825	215,040		£9	£25	£75	£150/£225
1825	Proof		--	---	---	£150/£300
1826	9,031,630 Rev A		£4	£9	£35	£65/£95
1826	Proof Rev A		--	--	---	----/£250
1826	Proof Rev A	bronzed		--	---	----/£180
1826	Rev B		£6	£20	£60	£120/£180
1826	Proof Rev B		--	--	£75	£200/£300
1826	Proof Rev B	bronzed		--	---	----/£180
1827	5,376,000		£4	£10	£50	£90/£125

Rev A; Saltire of shield has two incuse lines P1433
Rev B; Saltire of shield has one raised line P1436
The Saltire forms the cross of St. George/St. Andrew, often divided by line/s.

WILLIAM IV — BARE HEAD — COPPER 28mm

Date	Mintage		Fine	V.F.	E.F.	abt. Unc/FDC.
1831	806,400		£4	£10	£45	£95/£125
1831	Proofs, bronzed	head/tail reversed ↓				£200/----
1831	Proofs, bronzed	head/tail upright ↑				£300/----
1834	537,600		£4	£10	£45	£95/£125
1837	349,400		£3	£8	£35	£80/£120

VICTORIA Young Head DATE BELOW HEAD COPPER

Date	Mintage	Fine	V.F.	E.F.	abt. Unc/FDC.
1838	456,960	£1	£5	£25	£60/£95
1839	Proofs, bronzed	---	--	---	£125/£225
1839	Proofs, bronzed, inverted reverse, from the sets				£120/£250
1841	1,075,200	£1	£5	£20	£45/£75
1841	Ordinary issue, inverted reverse		£25	£100	£225/£350
1841	Proofs, bronzed	---	---	---	£90/---
1841	Proof, in silver, on thick flan (2.8mm)		"guesstimate"		£1500/£2000
1843	967,680	£5	£12	£45	£90/£130
1844	1,075,200	£3	£7	£30	£60/£85
1845	1,075,200	£20	£55	£175	£350/£475
1846	860,160	£4	£9	£40	£70/£95
1847	752,640	£4	£10	£45	£90/£135
1848	322,560	£10	£30	£90	£270/----
1848 *	8 struck over 7	---	£7	£25	£50/£75
1848	8 struck over 3	---	£12	£30	---/---
1851	215,040 (no dots)	---	£6	£25	£50/£75
1851	Shield, 7 incuse dots	---	£12	£50	£100/£150
1852	637,056 (no dots)	---	£6	£25	£50/£75
1852	Shield, 7 incuse dots	---	£12	£50	£100/£150
1853	1,559,040	£1	£5	£15	£45/£60
1853	3 over 2	£9	£18	£50	£150/----
1853	Proofs, bronzed, inverted reverse		---	---	£200/£300
1853	Copper proof (Colin Cooke 1993)				---/£150
1854	12,354,048 ?	£3	£6	£18	£40/£55
1855	1,455,837	£3	£6	£20	£60/£80
1856	1,942,080	£4	£9	£40	£80/£120
1857	1,182,720 (no dots)	---	£12	£50	£100/£150
1857	Shield, 7 incuse dots	---	£6	£25	£75/£125
1858	2,472,960	£1	£5	£20	£40/£75
1858	Smaller date	£2	£6	£30	£60/£90
1858	last 8 over 6	£4	£8	£25	£50/£75
1858	last 8 over 7	£3	£6	£20	£40/£65
1859	1,290,340	£8	£15	£45	£150/£200
1859	9 struck over 8	£6	£12	£40	£95/£130
1860 **	Extremely rare	£200	£500	£2500	£4000/---
1860 **	Extremely rare Proof	--	£1000	EF+ £2700	----

* Variety more common than correctly dated piece
** Date is below head, not below Britannia

VICTORIA "Bun" Head HALFPENNIES

DATE BELOW BRITANNIA — BRONZE 26 mm

Date	Mintage	Fine	V.F.	E.F.	abt. Unc/FDC.
TYPE 1: BEADED BORDERS :					
1860	1 + A (P1750)	£1	£5	£18	£30/£50
1860	noted (Cooke 1993)	"BU full lustre"		- - -	£34
1860	1 + A (P1751/52/53 Proofs bronze and bronzed £450 to £650				
1860	A "mule" (Coincraft 1995)	£200	£1000		Type1/Type2

TYPE 2: TOOTHED BORDERS :

Obv 2 has 7 berries. Obv 3 has 4 berries, all leaves have raised mid-ribs. Obv 4 has 4 berries, but four leaves have double incuse lines to mid-ribs.

Lighthouse : B tapering, pointed C cylindrical with rounded top.

Date	Mintage	Fine	V.F.	E.F.	abt. Unc/FDC.
1860	2 + B (P1754)	£1	£5	£20	£50/£80
1860	3 + B (P1756)	£1	£6	£25	£75/£100
1860	3 + C (P1757)	£1	£6	£25	£75/£100
1860	4 + B (P1758)	£4	£12	£30	£90/£120
1860★	F of HALF struck over P "VF" $60 (£25 1987) (The Rawcliffe Halfpenny)				
1860	(1996)	£25	£50	- - -	- - -/- - -
1861	54,118,400 Ten obv/rev combinations + proofs				
1861	Without signature	50p	£2	£10	£25/£40
1861	Signature on rock	£1	£3	£20	£50/£85
1862	61,107,200:				
	L.C.W. on rock	£1	£3	£10	£20/£30
1862	Proof P1775	- -	- -	- - -	£200
1862	No L.C.W. P1776	- -	£2	£8	£15/£25
1862	Proof P1777	- -	- - -	£200	- - -
1862	A, B, or C to left of lighthouse				£360/£500
1862	Unbarred A Le Λ	£120	- - -	- - -	- - -/- - -

★ FARTHINGS of this date bear Fs with little or no lower serif to the lower horizontal bar (illustr.) Perhaps the first halfpennies were struck with the same, or a similar, type-face and were overstruck to avoid having HALP PENNYs as well as PARTHINGS.

Date	Mintage	Fine	V.F.	E.F.	abt Unc/FDC
1863	15,948,800	£1	£5	£20	£45/£60
1864	537,600	£4	£9	£30	£60/£90
1865	8,064,000	£4	£12	£45	£90/£125
1865	5 over 3	£15	£60	£180	£360/£450
1866	2,508,800	£4	£10	£35	£70/£105
1867	2,508,806	£5	£12	£45	£90/£140
1868	3,046,400	£4	£10	£40	£80/£120
1868	Cupro-nickel proof	Noted 1993	(KB Coins)	"FDC"	£325
1869	3,225,600	£5	£25	£75	£150/£225
1870	4,350,739	£4	£9	£30	£60/£90
1871	1,075,280 ?	£15	£45	£145	£300/£450
1872	4,659,410	£1	£4	£24	£36/£55
1873	3,404,880	£1	£5	£25	£50/£75
1874	1,347,665	£3	£15	£55	£125/- - -
1874	Portrait as 1874H	£1	£4	£24	£35/£55
1874H	5,017,600	£1	£4	£20	£45/£65
1874H	Proof	Noted 1993	(Cooke)	"FDC"	£150
1875	5,430,815	£1	£2	£16	£35/£55
1875H	1,254,400	£3	£6	£25	£45/£65
1876H	6,809,600	£1	£2	£16	£30/£50
1877	5,209,505	£1	£2	£16	£35/£55
1878	1,425,535	£3	£12	£36	£85/£150
1879	3,582,545	£1	£2	£12	£30/£50
1880	2,423,465	£2	£5	£20	£30/£45
1881	2,007,515	£2	£5	£20	£30/£45
1881H	1,792,000	£1	£3	£15	£30/£50
1882H	4,480,000	£1	£3	£15	£20/£35
1883	Portrait as 1874 to 1882H		£15	£45	£90/- - -
1883	3,000,725	£3	£6	£25	£50/£75
1884	6,989,580	£1	£2	£12	£25/£40
1885	8,600,574	£1	£2	£12	£25/£40
1886	8,586,155	£1	£2	£10	£25/£40
1887	10,701,305	£1	£2	£9	£25/£40
1888	6,814,070	£1	£3	£12	£25/£40
1889	7,748,234	£1	£2	£12	£25/£40
1889	9 over 8	£8	£30	£90	£180/£260
1890	11,254,235	£1	£2	£10	£25/£35
1891	13,192,260	£1	£2	£10	£25/£40
1892	2,478,335	£2	£3	£10	£25/£35
1893	7,229,344	£1	£2	£9	£25/£35
1894	1,767,635	£1	£3	£10	£35/£50

HALFPENNIES

BRONZE 26mm

Date	Mintage	(Peck No.)	Fine	V.F.	E.F.	Unc/abt FDC
VICTORIA		**Veiled, Old, or Widow Head**				
1895	3,032,154	P1950	30p	£1	£4	£18/35
1896	9,142,500	P1951	25p	90p	£3	£12/£25
1897	8,690,315	P1951A	30p	£1	£4	£15/£30
1897	Horizon higher	P1952	---	90p	£3	£12/£20
1898	8,595,180	P1953	35p	£1	£4	£15/£20
1899	12,108,001	P1954	20p	60p	£3	£12/£18
1900	13,805,190	P1955	---	60p	£2	£6/£10
1901	11,127,360	P1956	---	---	£2	£6/£10
EDWARD VII						
1902	13,672,960		---	---	£3	£10/£15
1902	LOW TIDE variety		£2	£8	£32	£60/£90
1903	11,450,880		---	£1	£5	£15/£22
1904	8,131,200		---	£2	£8	£25/£30
1905	10,124,800		---	£1	£5	£22/£30
1906	11,101,440		---	£1	£4	£12/£20
1907	16,849,280		---	£1	£4	£12/£25
1908	16,620,800		---	£1	£5	£20/£28
1909	8,279,040		---	£1.50	£8	£20/£28
1910	10,769,920		---	£1	£5	£15/£20

Proofs exist for 1902; they are very rare.

"LOW TIDE" VARIETY referred to above and on page 14 may be determined thus: if the horizon meets Britannia at the point, below the knee, where right and left legs cross; NORMAL tide is indicated. If, however, the horizon meets Britannia at a much lower point - nearer the hem of her drape - then a LOW TIDE variety has been detected.

Date	Mintage	Fine	V.F.	E.F.	
GEORGE V		**BRITANNIA REVERSE**			
1911	12,570,880		£1	£3	[illegible]
1912	21,185,920		£1	£3	[illegible]
1913	17,476,480		£1	£5	[illegible]/£25
1914	20,289,111		£1	£4	£12/£20
1915	21,563,040		£1	£4	£12/£20
1916	39,386,143		70p	£4	£12/£20
1917	38,245,436	---	60p	£3	£12/£20
1918	22,321,072	---	60p	£3	£12/£20
1919	28,104,001	---	60p	£3	£12/£20
1920	35,146,793	---	60p	£3	£12/£20
1921	28,027,293	---	60p	£2	£10/£15
1922	10,734,964	---	£1.25	£4	£12/£20
1923	12,266,282	---	65p	£4	£12/£20
1924	13,971,038	---	65p	£4	£12/£20
1925	12,216,123 Head as for 1924		90p	£5	£15/£25
1925	Modified Head as for 1926		£1.50	£8	£12/£20
1926	6,712,306	---	£1	£6	£10/£15
1927	15,589,622	---	55p	£3	£10/£15
	SMALLER HEAD:				
1928	20,935,200	---	40p	£2	£4/£7
1928	Proof	---	(Spink 1988)		---/£175
1929	25,680,000	---	30p	£2	£4/£7
1930	12,532,800	---	30p	£2	£5/£8
1931	16,137,600	---	30p	£2	£5/£8
1932	14,448,000	---	30p	£2	£5/£8
1933	10,560,000	---	30p	£2	£5/£8
1934	7,704,000	---	40p	£2.50	£8/£12
1935	12,180,000	---	30p	£2	£5/£9
1935	(Cooke '95) (P2321) Bronze proof			"F.D.C."	£150
1936	23,008,800	---	---	£1	£3/£5

1911 Obverse 1a - the neck is hollow
Obverse 1b - the neck is flat
(See note on page 6)

Proofs 1926 to 1936 inclusive: British Museum.

1911 Some dies were punched with date close to line of exergue (segment containing date)

1912 A and B

Small gap = Rev A
Clear gap = Rev B

Combinations:
1a + A 1a + B
1b + A 1b + B

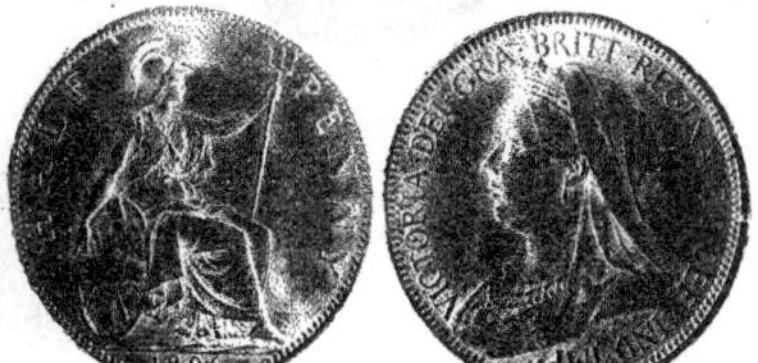

HALFPENNIES

Date	Mintage	Fine	V.F.	E.F.	Unc/abt. FDC
EDWARD VIII *(Duke of Windsor)*			Reverse GOLDEN HIND		
1937	Excessively rare	"Guesstimate"			£10,000/£15,000
GEORGE VI			Reverse GOLDEN HIND		
1937	24,504,000	---	---	65p	£1/£3
1937	26,402 proofs		---	---	£3/£5
1938	40,320,000	---	10p	£1	£2/£4
1938	Noted (D. Mason 1994) "BU 100% lustre"				--/£5
1939	28,924,800		10p	£1.50	£2/£4
1940	32,162,400		30p	£2	£3/£5
1941	45,120,000		5p	45p	£1/£3
1942	17,908,800		5p	45p	£1/£3
1943	76,200,000		10p	50p	£1/£3
1944	81,840,000		5p	45p	£1/£3
1945	57,000,000		5p	70p	£1.50/£3.50
1946	22,725,600		30p	£2	£3/£5
1947	21,266,400		10p	£1	£4/£6
1948	26,947,200	---	10p	45p	£1/£2
1949	24,744,000	---	10p	£1	£4/£6
1950	24,153,600	---	10p	45p	£2/£4
1950	17,513 proofs	---	---	---	£2.50/£4
1951	14,868,000	---	20p	£1.20	£4/£6
1951	20,000 proofs	---	---	---	£2.50/£4
1952	33,278,400	---	10p	25p	£1/£2

1940
* L * * P * = Rev A
* L * * P * = Rev B
* L = Rev C
See 'pointings' page 3

ELIZABETH II

Cross points BETWEEN rim beads = Obverse 1
Cross points TO a rim bead = Obverse 2

Date	Mintage	Fine	V.F.	E.F.	Unc/abt. FDC/FDC
1953	8,910,000:				
1953	Obverse 1	---	---	---	£3/£5
1953	Obverse 2	---	10p	20p	£1/£2
1953	40,000 proofs	---	---	---	£3/£6
1954	19,375,200	---	10p	£1	£3/£4/£6
1955	18,465,600	---	10p	£1	£2/£3/£5
1956	21,799,200	---	---	£1	£3/£4/£6
1957	39,672,000	---	---	20p	£1/£2/£3
1957	Variety has a calm sea	---	---	£2	£4/£5/£8
1958	66,331,200	---	---	---	50p/£1/£2
1958	Proof (noted 1994)	---	---	---	---/£75
1959	79,176,000	---	---	---	50p/£1/£2
1960	41,340,000	---	---	---	50p/£1/£2
1961	Decimal Patterns see page 43		---	---	---
1962	41,779,200	---	---	---	15p/50p/£2
1963	42,720,000	---	---	---	15p/40p/£2
1964	78,583,200	---	---	---	15p/30p/£1
1965	98,083,200	---	---	---	15p/30p/£1
1966	95,289,600	---	---	---	5p/15p/50p
1967	146,490,400 Narrow rim	---	---		5p/15p/50p
1967	Noted 1994 Wide rim (KB Coins)			"BU"	£2.50
	Total for 1967 includes 46,226,400 struck in 1968				
1970	750,424 LAST STERLING Proofs (1971/75)				£1/£2/£3

1925/27	Effigy modified to aid striking, all coins
1928	Smaller head, for halfpennies and pennies
1949	IND:IMP (Emperor of India) discontinued, all coins
1954	BRITT:OMN discontinued - all coins
1969	Halfpenny demonetized - 1st August

Date	Mintage	Peck No.	Fine	V.F.	E.F.	abt. Unc/FDC
GEORGE IV	***ROYAL (Tower) MINT***					COPPER 34mm
1825	1,075,200	P1420	£6	£20	£60	£125/£170
1825	Proofs		---	---	---	£200/£400
1826	5,913,000	P1422	£4	£15	£50	£95/£150
1826	(J. Welsh 1996)		---	---	"Gem · Unc"	£95
1826	St Andrew's Cross varieties:					
	Reverse B	Thin raised line		£20	£60	£125/£180
	Reverse C	Thick raised line		£25	£75	£150/£200
1826	Proofs: plain edged, bronzed			---	---	£150/£200
1826	Proofs: copper (unbronzed)			---	---	£300/£500
1827	1,451,520	Fair £20	£40	£120	£1250	£2500/£4000
1827	(noted 1991)	GVF - no corrosion £290				----
WILLIAM IV						COPPER 34mm
1831	806,400	P1455	£9	£40	£125	£250/£350
1831	Bronzed proofs		---	---	£90	£135/£200
1831	.W.W incuse initials on truncation			£45	£150	£300/£425
1831	W.W. incuse initials		---	£65	£200	£400/£500
1834	322,560	P1459	£10	£40	£130	£260/£400
1837	174,720	P1460	£12	£60	£200	£400/£500

Date	Mintage	Peck	Fine	V.F.	E.F.	Unc/FDC
VICTORIA Young Head		DATE BELOW HEAD 34mm				
1839	Bronzed proof	1479	DEF : o.t.		£150	£300/£450
1841	913,920 REG:	1480	£7	£20	£60	£150/£200
1841	Proofs		---	---	---	£250/£400
1841	Proof in silver	(1980	As Struck)		---	£1,500
1841	No colon REG	1484	£3	£6	£30	£60/£90
1843	483,830 REG:	1486	£20	£80	£300	£600/----
1843	No colon REG	1485	£30	£100	£400	£800/----
1844	215,040	1487	£4	£9	£40	£80/£120
1845	322,560	1489	£6	£18	£75	£150/£225
1846	483,840 DEF :	1490	£4	£10	£45	£100/£150
1846	DEF:	1491	£5	£15	£65	£125/£175
1847	430,080 DEF:	1492	£3	£10	£45	£95/£130
1847	DEF :	1493	£3	£10	£45	£95/£130
1848	161,280	1496	£3	£10	£45	£95/£130
1848	8 over 6	1494	--	£25	£75	£150/£225
1848	8 over 7	1495	--	£9	£45	£100/£145
1849	268,800	1497	£40	£125	£500	£1000/£1500
1851	432,224 DEF :	1498	£3	£10	£45	£90/£125
1851	DEF:	1499	£4	£12	£50	£120/£165
1853	1,021,440 DEF :	1500	£2	£6	£25	£40/£60
1853	Narrow date		---	---	£12	£20/£40
1853	Proofs - copper and bronzed				---	£250/£500
1853	DEF:	1503	£3	£8	£30	£75/£110
1853	Plain trident	1504	£3	£12	£30	£60/£90
1854	4 over 3	1505	£15	£45	£95	£135/£225
1854	6,720,000 p.t.	1506	£1	£7	£25	£50/£75
1854	Ornam trident	1507	£1	£6	£18	£35/£60
1855	5,273,866 o.t.	1508	£1	£7	£25	£50/£75
1855	Plain trident	1509	£1	£6	£20	£40/£60
1856	1,212,288 DEF:	p.t.	£12	£42	£150	£300/£400
1856	Plain trident proof	---	---	---	---	£250/£500
1856	DEF :	o.t.	£7	£35	£95	£250/£350
1857	752,640 DEF:	p.t.	£2	£6	£25	£50/£75
1857	DEF :	o.t.	£3	£8	£30	£60/£90
1857	Smaller date	p.t.	£2	£6	£25	£50/£75
1858	1,559,040:					
	8 over 3	1515	--	£22	£60	£90/---
	8 over 6		--	---	£60	---
	8 over 7	1516	--	£6	£25	£50/£75
	Smaller date	1517	£1	£6	£25	£50/£75
	Large date no W.W.	1518	£1	£5	£20	£40/£60
1859	1,075,200 Large date		£3	£8	£30	£60/£90
1859	9 over 8		£4	£16	£42	£95/£130
1859	Smaller date		£3	£9	£35	£80/£125
1859	Proof		---	---	---	£500/£750
1860	60 struck over 59		£100	£300	£600	£950/---

DEF: = near colon - DEF : = far colon - o.t. = ornamental trident
plain tridents have near colons p.t. = plain trident
All have ornamental tridents from 1839 to 1851

VICTORIA "Bun" Head PENNIES

1860 5,053,440 BEADED RIM BORDER

Obverse: L.C.WYON ON TRUNCATION

Rev	Peck		F.	V.F.	E.F.	Abt. Unc.
A	1617		£3	£6	£30	£60
B	1619		£6	£12	£45	£90
B	1620	extra heavy flan			£750	----
B	1620A	proof in gold (1987) £11,200				
B	1621	silv. proof			(£500 EF+)	
B	1622	bronzed proof			--	£500
C	1623		£10	£45	£95	---
Mule	1624	bead obv/tooth rev		£95	£250	£500
Mule	1628	tooth obv/bead rev		£250	£600	£1200

TOOTHED RIM/BORDER

Obverse: L.C.WYON ON or BELOW TRUNCATION

Rev	Peck		F.	V.F.	E.F.	Abt. Unc.
C★	1625	signature on		£9	£35	£70
C★		(S & B 1995) "gdEF much lustre"			£45	---
D	1626	signature on		£25	£95	£225
C★	1629	signature on		---	£35	£70
C★	1630	struck on heavy flan			£250	---
C★	1631	bronze proof		---		£250
C★	1632	signature below		£9	£35	£70
C★	1633	no signature		£50	£90	---
C★	1635	no signature		£50	£90	---
	1634	ONF PENNY variety: damaged die £35 fair (1988)				
	2051	Wyon Pattern MDCCCLX nickel-alloy (Seaby 1989 GEF £450)				

1861 36,449,280 :

Obverse: L.C.WYON ON or BELOW TRUNCATION

Rev	Peck		F.	V.F.	E.F.	Abt. Unc.
C★	1637	signature on		£120	---	---
F	1638	no signature		£75	---	---
C★	1639	sig. below	£2	£10	£25	£60
F	1642	no signature		£20	fair (1988)	
C★	1643	no sig	£35	---	---	---
C★	1644	no sig	---	---	£30	---
	6 over 8	Fair £50	£95	£225	---	---
F	1646	no sig		£5	£15	---

OBVERSE 5 - NO SIGNATURE - WREATH OF 16 LEAVES - RAISED MIDRIBS
REVERSE F - NO SIGNATURE - THUMB DOES NOT TOUCH ST.GEORGE'S CROSS

Date	Mintage	F.	V.F.	E.F.	abt.Unc.
1862	50,534,400	£1	£5	£25	£40
1862	Bronzed proof	---	---	---	£400
1862	Date from halfpenny die (smaller): Fair £60	£95	£250	---	----
1862	8 over 6 (Seaby 1989 GVF £275)				
1862	Pattern cu-nickel P2060 (FDC £600)				
1863	28,062,720	£1	£4	£20	£50
1863	Bronzed proof	---	---	---	£250
1863	Die number below date:				
	2 below £300 (Fine 1996)				
	3 below £100 (Fair 1988)				
	4 below £250 (Fine 1996)				
1864	3,440,646 Plain 4		£28	£125	£325
1864	Crosslet 4		£45	£200	£425
1864	(noted 1996)			"abtUnc"	£440

Date	Mintage	F.	V.F.	E.F.	Unc.
1865	8,601,600	£2	£9	£45	£90
1865	(noted 1996)	---	---	"abtUnc"	£65
1865	5 over 3	£25	£75	£300	£750
1865	Pattern P2061			"nrFDC"	£300
1866	9,999,360	£3	£10	£30	£60
1867	5,483,520	£4	£12	£35	£75
1868	1,182,720	£6	£20	£75	£150
1868	Bronze proof P1681			(1996)	£450
1868	Copper-nickel proof			£250	£400
1869	2,580,480	£30	£90	£300	£600
1870	5,695,022	£5	£15	£75	£150
1871	1,290,318	£15	£60	£200	£325
1872	8,494,572	£3	£12	£30	£75
1873	8,494,200	£3	£12	£30	£75

OBVERSE 5; and OBVERSE 6 (a MORE MATRONLY PORTRAIT)
REVERSE F; and REVERSE G (a LESS GRACEFUL BRITANNIA)

1874 5,621,86 :

O/R	Peck	F.	V.F.	E.F.	Unc.
5/F	1690	£5	£15	£50	£100
5/G	1691	£5	£15	£50	£100
6/F	1692	£3	£12	£40	£90
6/G	1693	£3	£12	£40	£90

1874H 6,666,240 :

O/R	Peck	F.	V.F.	E.F.	Unc.
5/F	1694	£4	£12	£45	£125
5/G	1695	£5	£16	£50	£150
6/F	1696	£4	£4	£45	£90
6/G	1697	£4	£4	£40	£85
6/G	1698	Bronze proof		---	£350

1860 reverse: L.C.W. incuse below shield
Rev. A = crosses outlined with treble incuse lines, no rock
Rev. B = crosses outlined by close, double, raised lines, no rock
Rev. C = similar to Rev. B, but small rock to left of lighthouse
Rev. C★ = as Rev. C, but with minor modifications to rocks and sea
Rev. D = as Rev. C, but L.C.W. incuse below foot
Rev. E = no signature, thumb touches St. George's Cross; no vertical lines to lantern
Rev. F = no signature, thumb does not touch Cross, lantern has six vertical lines
Rev. G = Britannia has long, thin neck; her helmet is tall and narrow; a tall, thin lighthouse

VICTORIA "Bun" Head (continued)

Date	Mintage	F.	V.F.	E.F.	Abt. Unc/FDC
1875	10,691,040	£2	£7	£25	£40/£60
1875H	752,640	£8	£45	£150	£300/£350
1875H	Proof P1706 (noted 1996)			"nr.FDC"	£450
1876H	11,074,560	£3	£9	£30	£60/---
1877	Narrow date	£200	---	---	---/---
1877	9,624,747	£2	£7	£25	£40/£75
1877	Proof cupro-nickel		---	"nr.FDC"	---/£700
1878	2,764,470	£3	£10	£30	£50/£75
1878	Proof P1713		---	"nr.FDC"	---/£275
1879	7,666,476	£2	£6	£24	£40/£55
1879	Narrow date	£10	£20	£60	£120/---
1879	Re-touched Obv. P1715			£75	"gdEF"
1880	3,000,831	£3	£10	£30	£55/£80
1880	Proof (noted 1996)		"abt.FDC"		---/£500
1881	2,302,261	£2	£10	£42	£65
1881	Portrait 'aged' further: P1722	£4	£15	£50	£75/£95
1881H	3,763,200	£2	£5	£16	£30/£45
1881H	Heraldically coloured shield				£50/---

Date	Mintage	F.	V.F.	E.F.	Unc.
1882H	7,526,400	£2	£6	£20	£40
1882	No H (beware removal)			£600	£900
1883	6,237,438	£2	£7	£25	£45
1884	11,702,802	£2	£5	£20	£40
1885	7,145,862	£2	£5	£20	£35
1886	6,087,759	£1	£4	£15	£30
1887	5,315,085	£1	£4	£15	£30
1887	Aluminium pattern (P2175)			---	£375
1888	5,125,020	£1	£4	£15	£30
1889	12,559,737	£1	£4	£14	£26
1889	Narrow date	(P1745)		£25	---
1890	15,330,840	£1	£4	£15	£30
1891	17,885,961	£1	£4	£15	£35
1892	10,501,671	£1	£4	£15	£30
1893	8,161,737	£1	£5	£16	£32
1894	3,883,452	£3	£6	£25	£45

Proofs for 1881, 1884/85/86 and 1890/91/92
All proofs except, perhaps, 1888 £350/£450

Old, Veiled, or Widow Head

Date	Mintage	F.	V.F.	E.F.	Unc.
1895	5,395,830	Rev B	£4	£12	£20
1895	No sea Rev A	£5	£20	£20	£175
1895	Pattern (P2066) (noted 1994)				£720
1896	24,147,156	£1	£3	£8	£16
1896	9 and 6 further apart		£5	£10	£25
1897	20,756,620	£1	£3	£6	£12
1897	Higher horizon		---	£100	£200
1898	14,296,836	£1	£3	£10	£20
1899	26,441,069	£1	£3	£6	£12
1900	31,778,109	---	£1	£4	£8
1900	Proofs	---	---	"FDC"	£300
1901	22,205,568	---	£1	£4	£8
1901	Proofs	---	---	"FDC"	£300

1895 Rev A, trident to P is 2mm; no sea behind
1895 Rev B, trident to P is 1mm; sea behind (to left of) Britannia

1895 Pattern, only five known, (1985 FDC) £1200
Full lustre and/or abt.FDC can add 50% to Unc. value

BRONZE 31 mm

PENNIES

Date	Mintage	Fine	V.F.	E.F.	abt. Unc/FDC
EDWARD VII					
1902	26,976,768	30p	£3	£5	£12/£20
1902	LOW TIDE variety	£1	£5	£20	£40/£60
1903	21,415,296	---	£4	£10	£20/£30
1903	Open '3' Fair £30 (Spink 1988)			---	---/---
1904	12,913,152	---	£5	£15	£25/£35
1905	17,783,808	---	£4	£12	£20/£30
1906	37,989,504	---	£4	£8	£15/£25
1907	47,322,240	---	£3	£9	£18/$24
1908	31,506,048	---	£3	£10	£20/£30
1909	19,617,024	---	£3	£9	£18/£24
1909	Noted 1994	(Cooke)	"BU Full Lustre 'blazing'"		£32
1909	(Coincraft 1995) lists a matt proof on thick flan @ £1,000				
1910	29,549,184	---	£3	£9	£18/£24
GEORGE V					
1911	23,079,168	(1 + A)	£4	£8	£15/£22
1911	Hollow neck	(see page 6)	(1988 GEF £20)		---
1912	48,306,048	(1 + A)	£3	£8	£15/£22
1912H	16,800,000	(1 + A)	£5	£20	£30/£45
1913	65,497,872	(2 + B)	£3	£6	£12/£20
1914	50,820,997	---	£3	£8	£15/£25
1915	47,310,807	---	£3	£5	£10/£15
1916	86,411,165	---	£2	£3	£9/£12
1917	107,905,436	---	£2	£3	£9/£12
1918	84,227,372	---	£2	£3	£6/£9
1918H	3,660,800	£1	£10	£70	£140/£200
1918KN	Inc above	£2	£15	£95	£200/£260
1919	113,761,090	---	£1	£5	£10/£15
1919H	5,209,600	£1	£10	£70	£140/£200
1919KN	Inc above	£2	£20	£100	£250/£300
1920	124,693,485	(2 + B)	£2	£5	£10/£20
1920	(P2259)	(3 + B)	---	---	---/---
1921	129,717,693	(2 + B)	£2	£5	£12/£22
1921	(P2261)	(3 + B)	£2	£5	£12/£22
1922	16,346,711	(3 + B)	£3	£15	£30/£50
1923 to 1925	None	---	---	---	---
1926	4,498,519	---	£5	£25	£50/£100
1926	Modified effigy	£3	£20	£200	£450/£650
1927	60,989,561	---	£2	£4	£6/£10
1928	50,178,000 smaller head		£2	£4	£6/£10
1929	49,132,800	---	£1	£5	£7/£12
1930	29,097,600	---	£1	£6	£9/£15
1931	19,843,200	---	£1	£7	£14/£21

Toothed circle of rev A has 163 teeth whilst B has 188

Obverse 1: bottom stop of colon close to A; GRA: BRITT
Obverse 2: stops are midway but cramped; GRA:BRITT
Obverse 3: as obverse 2 but words farther apart; GRA : BRITT :

Date	Mintage	Fine	V.F.	E.F.	abt. Unc/FDC
1932	8,277,600	---	£3	£15	£30/£45
1932	Proof (P2278)	(noted 1996)		"nr.FDC"	£250
1933	7 or 8 plus "patterns"			(Spink 1994)	£25,300
1933	Pattern by Lavrillier			(1986)	£4,100
1933	A uniface		(1980 £28,750)		£50,000
1934	13,965,600	---	£2	£9	£20/£30
1935	56,070,000	---	£1	£3	£4/£8
1935	Bronze proof	(noted 1995)		"FDC"	£220
1936	154,296,000	---	£1	£2	£3/£5

Proofs for all dates from 1926 to 1936 except 1933

In addition to the 7, possibly 8, pennies listed at left (left-hand pair above); there were patterns, possibly four, struck from dies engraved by André Lavrillier (right-hand pair above) having a 'military' King George V, a thick trident and a sea of wavy lines. Yet another 1933 penny is uniface: having a "tail" but the "head" replaced by the word MODEL. The 1933 set from St. Mary's Church, Hawksworth Wood, was offered for sale at Sotheby's in 1972. It fetched £7,000. This set was one of those placed under foundation stones laid by King George in 1933.

Bronze 31 mm

PENNIES

Date	Mintage	Fine	V.F.	E.F.	abt. Unc/FDC
EDWARD VIII (Duke of Windsor)					
1937	Specimen strikings only		"guesstimate"	from	£15,000
GEORGE VI					
1937	88,896,000	---	25p	50p	£1/£2
1937	26,402 proofs	---	---	---	/£5
1938	121,560,000	---	10p	65p	£2/£3
1939	55,560,000	---	30p	£1	£3/£5
1940	42,284,400	---	50p	£2	£6/£9
1941 to 1943	none	---	---	---	---
1944	42,600,000	---	30p	£2	£4/£6
1945	79,531,200	---	25p	£1.50	£3/£5
1945	Doubled 9	£1	£5	£25	---
1946	66,855,600	---	15p	£1	£2/£3
1947	52,220,400	---	15p	£1	£2/£3
1948	63,961,200	---	5p	25p	£1/£3
1948	(noted 1996)	---	---	"BU"	£4
1949	14,324,400	---	10p	60p	£1/£2
1950	240,000	£2	£4	£6	£12/£18
1950	17,513 proofs	---	---	---	/£15
1951	120,000	£3	£6	£9	£18/£25
1951	(noted 1996)	---	---	"BU"	£20
1951	20,000 proofs	---	---	---	£12/£15

Proofs for all dates except, possibly, 1947 ●●●●

1937	Rev Aa	Ns point to border teeth N N ●●●●
1937	Rev Ab	Ns point between teeth (b is rarer) N N
1940	Rev Ab	has single exergue line
1940	Rev B	has double exergue line (Ab is rarer)
1944	Rev Ba	waves touch exergue
1944	Rev Bb	gap between waves and exergue

(POINTINGS - page 3)

Date	Mintage	Fine	V.F.	E.F.	Unc/FDC
ELIZABETH II					
1953	Pattern (not in Peck) unique ? : has toothed (not beaded) border Spink				£1,950
1953	1,308,400 (from the 'Plastic' Set)			£1	£2/£4
1953	(noted 1996)	---	"BU. Full lustre"		£5
1953	40,000 proofs	---	---		£5/£6
1953	Pattern from sand-blasted dies		---	£300	(1985)
1954	1 retrieved from change.		Now in British Museum.		
1954	It is believed there are others		"guesstimate"		£21,000
1955 to 1960	none	---	---	---	---
1961	48,313,400	---	---	---	25p/60p
1962	157,588,600	---	---	---	20p/50p
1963	119,733,600	---	---	---	---/25p
1964	153,294,000	---	---	---	12p/25p
1965	121,310,400	---	---	---	10p/20p
1965	In gold, unofficial,	(Christies 1989)		---	£1300
1966	165,739,200	---	---	---	---/25p
1966	2 (so far) Jersey penny obverse.	(Auction 1992)			£605
1967	155,280,000	---	---	---	---/15p
1968	170,400,000 all dated 1967	(noted 1996)		"Full lustre"	20p
1969	219,360,000 all dated 1967				
1970	109,524,000 all dated 1967:	654,564,000			
	Proofs for some dates. 1970 proofs, from sets,				£1/£2

For a coin valued/costing less than £1, it should be borne in mind that almost ALL the value/cost lies in the handling, listing and storing of that coin. Whilst it enables collections to be expanded; such a small sum, even multiplied by many coins, is unlikely to be recoverable by re-selling. A long life, however, could make all the difference and we wish you exactly that!

THREE HALFPENCES

ISSUED FOR COLONIAL USE

Date	Mintage	Fine	V.F.	E.F.	abt. Unc/FDC
WILLIAM IV		SILVER 12 mm			
1834	800,448	£3	£6	£15	£25/£40
1835	633,600	£4	£7	£20	£30/£50
1835	5 struck over 4	£3	£9	£27	£40/£60
1836	158,400	£3	£6	£18	£36/£55
1837	30,624	£8	£20	£70	£120/£180
VICTORIA		SILVER 12 mm			
1838	538,560	£1	£5	£15	£25/£40
1839	760,320	£1	£5	£15	£25/£40
1840	95,040	£2	£10	£30	£60/£90
1841	158,400	£2	£6	£18	£35/£50
1842	1,869,120	£2	£7	£21	£40/£60
1843	475,200	£1	£4	£12	£25/£40
1843	43 over 34	£5	£12	£25	£50/£75
1843	43 over 34 (noted 1996)		"EF+"	£27	---/---
1860	160,000	£2	£10	£30	£60/£90
1862	256,000	£2	£10	£30	£60/£90
1862	Proof	(Seaby 1990)	abt.FDC		£475
1870	Proof, or pattern	(1986)	---	---	£325
1870	Proof, or pattern	(1996)	---	---	£750

THREEPENCES

Date	Mintage	Fine	V.F.	E.F.	abt. Unc/FDC
GEORGE IV				SILVER · 17 mm	
1822	small head (from Maundy 2d)	£3	£9	£18	£36/£45
1822	from Maundy proof set		---	---	---/---
1823	larger 'normal' head	£1	£6	£12	£24/£36
1824		£1	£6	£12	£24/£36
1825		£1	£6	£12	£24/£36
1826		£2	£10	£30	£50/£75
1826	(noted 1996)	--	"nr.EF"	£27	---/---
1827		£1	£6	£12	£24/£36
1828		£1	£6	£12	£24/£36
1828	from Maundy proof set		---	---	---/---
1829		£3	£9	£18	£36/£45
1830		£2	£8	£16	£30/£40
WILLIAM IV				SILVER 17 mm	
1831	from Maundy set	£1	£10	£20	£30/£50
1831	from proof set	--	---	---	£50/£65
1832	from Maundy set	£1	£10	£20	£21/£36
1833	from Maundy set	£1	£10	£20	£21/£36
For use in West Indies - unpolished surface:					
1834	401,016	£3	£15	£35	£70/£100
1835	491,040	£3	£15	£30	£65/£95
1836	411,840	£3	£15	£35	£70/£90
1837	42,768	£5	£20	£45	£90/£125

NOTE ON BULLION VALUE. Although the collector's value of a worn coin is listed as face-value-only (---), a silver one may have a higher, bullion value because of the precious metal in it. At one time pre 1947 silver coins were worth 4 times face value and pre 1920 ones up to 7 or 8 times. Buyers now make quotations on a day-to-day basis. A large enough quantity to sell is necessary to offset the cost of mailing. Check rates on Teletext. Be sure to contact the dealer before sending. "Travelling Dealers" offers in 1996 averaged £3 per £1 face value pre-1947 and £6 per £1 face-value for pre-1920; you would need to attend one of the ONE DAY ONLY events advertised in your local newspaper.

VICTORIA Young Head as Maundy but 'dull' surface

Date	Mintage	Fine	V.F.	E.F.	abt. Unc/FDC.
1838	1,203,840	£3	£6	£30	£60/£90
1839	570,240	£3	£9	£45	£90/£120
1840	633,600	£3	£9	£45	£90/£120
1841	443,520	£4	£10	£45	£90/£120
1842	2,027,520	£4	£10	£45	£90/£120
1843	included above	£2	£6	£30	£60/£95
1844	1,045,400	£$	£10	£40	£80/£110
Preceding coins were for use only in the colonies.					
1845	1,314,720	£3	£9	£35	£70/£100
1846	47,520	£15	£30	£120	£250/---
1849	126,720	£4	£12	£50	£75/£100
1850	950,400	£4	£10	£25	£50/£80
1851	479,065	£4	£10	£30	£60/£100
1851	(Coincraft Cat '95)	£50	£100	£250	---/---
1853	31,680	£15	£30	£120	£200/---
1854	1,467,246	£4	£8	£30	£50/£75
1855	383,350	£4	£9	£35	£80/---
1856	1,013,760	£4	£9	£35	£80/---
1857	1,758,240	£4	£9	£35	£80/---
1858	1,441,440	£4	£8	£35	£70/£95
1858	BRITANNIAB	£30	£120	£250	(error)
1859	3,579,840	£3	£6	£25	£35/£60
1860	3,405,600	£4	£9	£35	£60/£95
1861	3,294,720	£3	£6	£25	£45/£70
1862	1,156,320	£3	£8	£30	£60/£90
1863	950,400	£3	£8	£30	£65/£95
1864	1,330,560	£3	£6	£25	£40/£60
1865	1,742,400	£3	£8	£35	£70/£95
1866	1,900,800	£3	£6	£25	£40/£60
1867	712,800	£3	£7	£30	£50/£75
1868	1,457,280	£3	£6	£25	£40/£60
1868	RRITANNIAR	£20	£60	£200	error
1868	Laureate Head pattern by Wyon				---/---
1869	Colonial only	(noted 1993)		"abtFDC"	£250
1869	(Mason 1994)	--	£35	---	---/---

VICTORIA Young Head

Date	Mintage	Fair/Fine	V.F.	E.F.	abt. Unc/FDC
1870	1,283,218	£1/£3	£6	£25	£35/£60
1871	999,633	£1/£3	£6	£30	£45/£70
1872	1,293,271	£1/£3	£6	£30	£45/£70
1873	4,055,550	£1/£3	£5	£15	£30/£45
1874	4,427,031	£1/£3	£5	£15	£30/£45
1875	3,306,500	£1/£3	£5	£15	£30/£45
1876	1,834,389	£1/£3	£5	£15	£30/£45
1877	2,622,393	£1/£3	£5	£15	£30/£45
1878	2,419,975	£1/£3	£5	£15	£30/£45
1879	3,140,265	£1/£3	£5	£15	£30/£45
1880	1,610,069	£1/£3	£6	£18	£35/£50
1881	3,248,265	£1/£3	£6	£18	£35/£50
1882	472,965	£1/£4	£6	£25	£45/£70
1883	4,365,971	£1/£3	£5	£15	£30/£45
1884	3,322,424	£1/£3	£5	£15	£30/£45
1885	5,183,653	£1/£3	£5	£15	£30/£45
1886	6,152,669	£1/£3	£5	£15	£30/£45
1887	2,780,761 Yg Hd	£1/£3	£5	£15	£30/£45
	Young Head proof		---	---	£200/--

Jubilee Head

Date	Mintage	Fair/Fine	V.F.	E.F.	abt. Unc/FDC
1887	Included above	£2	£4	£6	£8/£12
1887	Jubilee Head proof	---	---		£35/£45
1888	518,199	£2	£4	£8	£15/£25
1889	4,587,010	£2	£4	£6	£12/£20
1890	4,465,834	£2	£4	£6	£12/£20
1891	6,323,027	£2	£4	£6	£12/£20
1892	2,578,226	£2	£4	£6	£12/£20
1893	3,067,243 Jub Hd	£5	£20	£35	£70/£100

Old or Widow Head

Date	Mintage	Fair/Fine	V.F.	E.F.	abt. Unc/FDC
1893	Included above	£2	£4	£6	£12/£18
1893	1,312 Proofs	--	---	---	£40/£60
1894	1,608,603	£3	£5	£8	£15/£20
1895	4,788,609	£3	£5	£8	£15/£20
1896	4,598,442	£3	£5	£8	£15/£20
1897	4,541,294	£2	£4	£6	£12/£18
1898	4,567,177	£2	£4	£6	£12/£18
1899	6,246,281	£2	£4	£6	£12/£18
1900	10,644,480	£2	£4	£6	£12/£18
1901	6,098,400	£1	£3	£5	£10/£15

* Threepences bearing dates not listed are, probably, Maundy pieces.

SILVER THREEPENCES

EDWARD VII

SILVER 16mm

Date	Mintage	Fine	V.F.	E.F.	abt. Unc/FDC
1902	8,268,480	£1	£2	£3	£5/£8
1902	15,123 proofs	---	---		£10/£15
1903	5,227,200	£2	£3	£12	£18/£25
1904	3,627,360	£3	£8	£20	£40/£50
1905	3,548,160	££	£8	£18	£30/£40
1906	3,152,160	£2	£8	£12	£24/£36
1907	4,831,200	£1	£3	£9	£15/£25
1908	8,157,600	£2	£4	£12	£20/£30
1909	4,055,040	£2	£4	£12	£20/£30
1910	4,563,380	£1	£3	£9	£15/£25

GEORGE V

SILVER (.925 to 1920 then .500) 16mm

Date	Mintage	Fine	V.F.	E.F.	abt. Unc/FDC
1911	5,841,084	75p	£2	£3	£6/£10
1911	6,001 proofs	---	---		£20
1912	8,932,825	60p	£1	£2	£6/£9
1913	7,143,242	60p	£1	£2	£6/£9
1914	6,733,584	60p	£1	£2	£6/£9
1915	5,450,617	60p	£2	£4	£8/£15
1916	18,555,201	60p	£1	£3	£5/£8
1917	21,662,490	60p	£1	£2	£3/£5
1918	20,630,909	60p	£1	£2	£3/£5
1919	16,845,687	60p	£1	£2	£3/£5
1920	16,703,597	50p	£1	£2	£4/£6
1920	.500 silver	50p	£1	£2	£4/£6
1921	8,749,301	50p	£1	£2	£3/£5
1922	7,979,998	50p	£1	£4	£8/£12
1923	Small number of patterns, struck in nickel			--	--
1925	3,731,859	£1	£2	£6	£12/£18
1925	Patterns, in nickel, of new (1927) design			--	--
1926	4,107,910	£1	£3	£12	£22/£36
1926	Modified Effigy (page 23)	50p	£1.50	£6	£12/£18

1904 Large '3' closer to bow at bottom and crown at top.
1911 Obv. 1a = neck hollow } as described on page 6.
Obv. 1b = neck flat

GEORGE V

SILVER (50%) 16mm

Date	Mintage	Fine	V.F.	E.F.	abt. Unc/FDC
1927	15,022 proofs oak sprig/acorn reverse			--	£25/£35
1928	1,302,106	75p	£2	£5	£10/£15
1929	None	---	---	---	---/---
1930	1,319,412	50p	£1	£5	£10/£15
1930	(noted 1996)	---	---	"FDC"	---/£20
1931	6,251,936	50p	£1	£2	£2/£4
1932	5,887,325	50p	£1	£2	£2/£4
1933	5,578,541	50p	£1	£2	£2/£4
1934	7,405,954	50p	£1	£2	£4/£6
1934	A proof offered for sale in 1976 (!)				/£55
1934	Proof (now listed in Coincraft 1995)			---	£260
1935	7,027,654	25p	50p	£1	£2/£3
1936	3,238,670	25p	50p	£1	£2/£3

EDWARD VIII (Duke of Windsor)

1937 Pattern bearing a design of three rings "guesstimate" £9500/£12000

GEORGE VI

SILVER (50%) 16mm

Date	Mintage	Fine	V.F.	E.F.	abt. Unc/FDC
1937	8,148,156	25p	50p	£1	£2/£3
1937	26,402 proofs	---	---	---	£3/£5
1938	6,402,473	25p	50p	£1	£2/£3
1939	1,355,860	25p	50p	£2	£4/£6
1940	7,914,401	25p	50p	£1	£2/£3
1941	7,979,411	25p	50p	£1	£2/£3
1942	4,144,051 Colonial	£1	£2	£5	£9/£15
1943	1,379,220 Colonial	£1	£3	£6	£10/£16
1944	2,005,553 Colonial	£2	£6	£10	£15/£20
1945	371,000 dated 1944; re-melted by The Mint				

One dated 1945 is known to have 'escaped'. (Coincraft '95 VF £4,000)

ELIZABETH II

Date	Mintage	Fine	V.F.	E.F.	abt. Unc/FDC
1953	Maundy Silver 3d	--	£25	£30	£60/---
1954 to 1995		--	£8	£12	£15/---

EDWARD VIII Duke of Windsor

Date	Mintage	Fine	V.F.	E.F.	Unc/abt FDC
1937	Date divided by THRIFT PLANT (Sea-pink); a few were made for slot machine testing and thicknesses vary.		Spinks (1990)		£28.500
			Cooke (1994)		£24.500
1937	Date at bottom, but effigy Edward VIII. Certainly rarer than that listed above. Lettering is EDWARDVS VIII *not* GEORGVS VI.				

GEORGE VI DODECAGONAL - MODIFIED THRIFT PLANT

Date	Mintage	Fine	V.F.	E.F.	Unc/abt FDC
1937	45,707,957	---	50p	£1	£2/£3
1937	(Welsh 1996)	---	---	"Gem, BU/FDC"	--/£4
1937	26,402 proofs	---	---	---	£4/£6
1938	14,532,332	5p	30p	£3	£6/£9
1939	5,603,021	12p	60p	£4	£15/£20
1940	12,636,018	10p	50p	£2	£4/£6
1941	60,239,489	---	50p	£1	£2/£3
1942	103,214,400	---	50p	£1	£2/£3
1943	101,702,400	---	50p	£1	£2/£3
1944	69,760,000	---	50p	£1	£2/£3
1945	33,942,466	---	50p	£2	£3/£6
1946	620,734	£1	£5	£40	£125/£175
1946	(noted 1994)	---	"gd E.F."	£67	----/----
1946	Proof "FDC"	(1985)	£250	---	(1996) £350
1947	None	---	---	---	---
1948	4,230,400	12p	£1	£5	£10/£15
	IND. IMP discontinued				
1949	464,000	£2	£6	£45	£95/£150
1949	A proof in brass	---	---	---	£200/£400
1950 }*	1,600,000	10p	£2	£10	£20/£40
1950 }*	17,513 proofs	---	---	---	£10/£15
1951	1,184,000	10p	£2	£10	£20/£40
1951	20,000 proofs	---	---	---	£20/£25
1952	25,494,400	---	50p	£1	£2/£4

British Museum has proof/s of each date

1937 Two different spacings from rim of word THREE noted :
Rev. A = large gap; Rev. B = small gap

* A "Strange Madness" when a superb proof striking costs less than one struck for general circulation.

Sharp v Rounded Corners:
1937 - 1940 All sharp
1941 - Both
1942 - 1946 All rounded
1948 - Both
1949 - All rounded
1950 - 1952 All sharp

ELIZABETH II

PORTCULLIS with CHAINS, ROYALLY CROWNED

Date	Mintage		Fine	V.F.	E.F.	abt. Unc/FDC
1953	30,618,000	BRITT.OMN		25p	50p	75p/£1.50
1953	40,000	proofs Obv.2		---	---	£2/£4
1954	41,720,000	no BRITT.OMN		25p	50p	£2/£4
1954	Matt proof		(1982 - Seaby)			£90
1955	41,075,200		---	25p	50p	£1/£2
1956	36,801,600		---	45p	£1	£2/£4
1957	24,294,400		---	25p	£1.50	£3/£6
1958	20,504,000		---	45p	£1	£4/£8
1958	Proof		(Coincraft 1993)		FDC	£275
1959	28,499,200		---	---	50p	£2/£3
1960	83,078,400		---	---	25p	£1/£2
1961	41,102,400		---	---	20p	40p/95p
1962	51,545,600		---	---	20p	40p/95p
1963	35,280,000		---	---	20p	40p/95p
1964	44,867,200		---	---	10p	20p/50p
1965	27,160,000		---	---	10p	20p/50p
1966	53,760,000		---	---	10p	20p/50p
1967	151,780,800		---	---	5p	10p/25p
1970	750,476	proofs for LAST STERLING set			F.D.C.	£3
	Undated error - double obverse ("heads" both sides)					£350

V.A.T., not included here, is sometimes absorbed by the seller on a 'special offer' basis.

1953 (a) = I of ELIZABETH points to corner of rim/edge.
(b) = I is much further to the right (see page 3).

1953 Obv. 1 Details, particularly head ribbon and initials M.G. are poorly defined = ex-specimen set (page 48).
Obv. 2 Portrait more sharply outlined as are the ends of the head ribbon = normal issue.
Both have ovoid stops.

1954 Much sharper overall and with round stops.

FOURPENCES or GROATS

WILLIAM IV

Reverse has FOUR PENCE in words - SILVER 16mm

Date	Mintage	Fair/Fine	V.F.	E.F.	abt. Unc./FDC
1836	Britannia seated : D :	£1/£3	£5	£15	£30/£40
1836	Colons close to :D:	£5	£10	£20	---/---
1836	Proofs, grained (milled) edge in silver			---	---/---
1836	Proofs, plain edge in gold	(Coincraft Cat '95)			£4,000
1836	Proofs, plain edge in silver		---	£275	---/£350
1837	962,280	£1/£4	£6	£18	£30/£45

A number of patterns exist

The FOURPENCE, not the silver threepence, is the true "Joey": taking its name from one Joseph Hume who recommended it to facilitate payment of the, then, 4d London omnibus fare.

VICTORIA

FOUR PENCE in words - SILVER 16mm

Date	Mintage	Fine	V.F.	E.F.	abt. Unc/FDC
1837	Proof only - plain edged		---		---/£1200
1837	Proof only - grained (milled) edge			---	---/£1200
1838	2,150,280	£2	£6	£18	£36/£50
1838	2nd 8 struck over ∞	£5	£10	£30	£60/£95
1838	Plain edged proof	---	---	---	£150
1839	1,461,240	£2	£6	£18	£36/£50
1839	Plain edged proof from the sets			---	£150
1840	1,496,880	£2	£6	£18	£36/£50
1840	(Mason 1994)	"1840 over O · gd.VF £12 · Unrecorded overdate"			
1841	344,520	£4	£8	£20	£40/£60
1841	Second 1 over I	£4	£8	£20	£40/£60
1842	724,680	£2	£3	£12	£36/£50
1842	Plain edged proof	---	---	---	£200
1842	2 struck over 1	£5	£10	£50	--/----
1843	1,817,640	£2	£6	£18	£36/£54
1844	855,360	£2	£6	£20	£50/£70
1845	914,760	£2	£6	£20	£50/£65
1846	1,366,200	£1	£5	£20	£50/£65
1847	7 struck over 6	£15	£60	£240	---/----
1848	712,800	£5	£10	£20	£40/£60
1848	2nd 8 over 6	£6	£12	£30	£60/£80
1848	2nd 8 over 7	£6	£15	£40	£75/£95
1849	380,160	£4	£9	£25	£40/£60
1849	9 struck over 8	£5	£10	£30	£60/£80
1851	594,000	£15	£50	£150	£300/----
1852	31,300	£25	£90	£200	£400/----
1853	11,880	£30	£120	£300	£600/----
1853	Grained (milled) edge proof from set			---	£300
1853	Plain edged proof	(noted 1996) "EF"		£150	----
1854	1,096,613	£2	£5	£15	£25/£36
1854	5 struck over 3	£2	£5	£18	£35/£55
1855	646,041	£2	£5	£16	£32/£45
1857	Proof only, grained edge		---	---	£650
1862	Proof only, plain edge		---	---	£450
1888	JUBILEE HEAD (Br.Guiana)	£4	£8	£25	£50/£65
1888	Grained edge proof	---	---	---	£400/£500

GEORGE IV

Date	Mintage/etc	Fine	V.F.	E.F.	Unc/abt. FDC
1820	Proof only, garnished shield		---		£600/£750
1821	863,280	£5	£15	£30	£60/£100
1821	Proof (ESC 1655) ---	---	---	---	£350/----
1821	BBITANNIAR error	£30	£90	£350	£700/£950
1824	633,600 gartered shield	£6	£18	£60	£120/£170
1825	483,120 gartered shield	£5	£15	£50	£110/£160
1825	Pattern for BARE HEAD design (Spink)			---	£2,000
1826	689,040	£10	£40	£125	£250/£325
1826	A proof - Shield within Garter ---			---	£125
1826	(KB Coins 1995) "Very Rare FDC"			---	£125
	Type change to BARE HEAD - LION on CROWN reverse				
1826	Included above	£4	£12	£36	£50/ £75
1826	A proof - Bare Head/Lion on Crown				£125/£200
1827	166,320	£12	£30	£80	£165/£220
1828	15,840 ?	£8	£24	£65	£125/----
1829	403,920	£6	£15	£60	£100/----

WILLIAM IV

SILVER 19mm

Date	Mintage/etc	Fine	V.F.	E.F.	Unc/abt. FDC
1831	1,340,195	£4	£12	£30	£75/ £95
1831	A proof - plain edge	---	---	---	£75/ £95
1834	5,892,480	£4	£15	£40	£90/£130
1835	1,552,320	£4	£15	£40	£90/£130
1836	1,987,920	£10	£25	£85	£120/----
1837	506,880	£6	£18	£60	£120/£180

VICTORIA Young Head

Date	Mintage/etc	Fine	V.F.	E.F.	abt. Unc/FDC
1838	1,607,760	£4	£12	£45	£75/£110
1839	3,310,560	£4	£15	£50	£75/£120
1839	A proof or pattern	---	---	---	£145/£160
1840	2,098,800	£5	£9	£38	£75/£110
1840	Pattern by W.Wyon rev cancelled with fine lines				---/ ---
1841	1,386,000	£5	£18	£60	£95/£150
1841	Pattern, gold, using half-sovereign reverse				
1842	601,920	£5	£18	£60	£90/£130
1843	3,160,080	£4	£15	£50	£80/£120
1844	3,975,840	£4	£12	£40	£70/£100
1844	Has large 44	£5	£15	£50	£90/£140
1845	3,714,480	£4	£15	£50	£90/£140
1846	4,268,880	£4	£10	£40	£60/ £90
1848	586,080	£25	£75	£250	£500/ ---
1848	8 struck over 6	---	£75	£250	£500/ ---
1848	8 struck over 7	---	£75	£250	£500/ ---
1850	498,960	£5	£15	£50	£150/ ---
1850	5 struck over 3 (Cooke 1990)	---		"abtBU"	£99/ ---
1851	2,288,107	£4	£15	£50	£90/£125
1852	904,586	£4	£15	£50	£90/£125
1853	3,837,930	£4	£15	£45	£80/£120
1853	A proof	---	---	---	£300
1854	840,116	£45	£200	£500	£1000/£1500
1855	1,129,084	£4	£15	£45	£90/£125
1855	A proof	---	---	---	£250
1856	2,779,920	£4	£15	£45	£95/£125
1856	A pattern worded	HALF	SHILLING		----
1856	A pattern worded	1/2	SHILLING		----
1857	2,233,440	£4	£12	£40	£80/£120
1858	1,932,480	£4	£12	£40	£80/£120
1858	A Proof	---	---	---	£250
1859	4,688,640	£4	£12	£45	£90/£125
1859	9 struck over 8	(Spink 1988 GEF £145)			---/ ---
1860	1,100,880	£4	£12	£42	£75/£120
1862	990,000	£25	£75	£250	£500/ ---
1863	491,040	£12	£45	£125	£250/£375
	NOW WITH DIE NUMBER (above date, below wreath)				
1864	4,253,040	£4	£12	£45	£90/£125
1865	1,631,520	£4	£15	£50	£100/£150
1866	5,140,080	£4	£12	£45	£90/£125
1866	No die number	£25	£95	£350	----/----
1867	1,362,240	£6	£18	£60	£95/ ---
1867	A proof	---	---	---	£250
1868	1,069,200	£6	£20	£65	£95/£145
1869	388,080	£6	£20	£65	£95/£145
1869	A proof	---	---	---	£500/----

1856 Variety: longer line below PENCE - rare
1857 Variety: longer line below PENCE - rare

SIXPENCES

VICTORIA (continued) *DIE NUMBER above date, below wreath*

Date	Mintage	Fine	V.F.	E.F.	Unc/abt. FDC
1870	479,613	£5	£16	£65	£120/£150
1870	A proof	---	---	---	£155
1871	3,662,684	£2	£8	£25	£50/ £80
1871	A proof (noted 1996)	"Plain edged Uncirc."			£800/---
1871	No die number	£3	£15	£50	£100/£150
1871	A proof without die number	---		---	£225/£350
1872	3,382,048 die no.	£4	£10	£30	£60/ £90
1873	4,594,733 die no.	£4	£10	£30	£60/ £90
1874	4,225,726 die no.	£4	£10	£30	£60/ £90
1875	3,256,545 die no.	£4	£10	£30	£60/ £90
1876	841,435 die no.	£5	£12	£50	£90/£120
1877	4,066,486 die no.	£4	£10	£40	£75/£100
1877	No die number	£4	£10	£40	£75/£100
1878	2,624,525 die no.	£4	£10	£40	£75/£100
1878	A proof of previous coin	---	---	---	£250/£400
1878	8 struck over 7 (die no.)	£8	£25	£35	£150/----
1878	DRITANNIAR error	£25	£75	£225	£375/£575
1879	3,326,313	£4	£12	£40	£70/£100

DIE NUMBERS DISCONTINUED

Date	Mintage	Fine	V.F.	E.F.	Unc/abt. FDC
1879	Included above	£4	£12	£35	£55/ £85
1879	A proof	---	---	---	£200/£400
1880	Hair lock on cheek	£8	£15	£50	£100/£150
1880	No lock of hair ★	£4	£12	£45	£90/£120
1880	No lock of hair ★ ★	(Cooke 1991)	"abt. BU"		---/ £50
	★ ★ The reverse of this example has smaller lettering than ★				
1880	A proof	---	---	---	£150/£300
1881	6,239,447	£4	£12	£35	£65/ £95
1881	A proof	---	---	---	£175/£250
1882	759,809	£6	£15	£40	£75/£100
1883	4,986,558	£4	£12	£35	£65/ £95
1884	3,422,565	£4	£10	£30	£60/ £90
1884	Pattern bearing national emblems	---		---	£600
1885	4,652,771	£4	£12	£35	£50/ £80
1886	2,728,249	£4	£12	£35	£50/ £80
1886	A proof	---	---	---	£175/£200
1887	3,675,607 Young Head	£4	£12	£35	£70/£100
1887	A proof Young Head	---	---	---	£120/£175

First Young Head 1838 to 1860 inclusive.
Second Young Head 1867 to 1880; as first but lower relief.
Third Young Head 1880 to 1887; Reverse has larger letters.

---A---

---B---

VICTORIA Jubilee Head

Reverse --A-- GARTERED SHIELD 'WITHDRAWN':

Date	Mintage	Fine	V.F.	E.F.	abt. Unc/FDC
1887	3,675,607	£1	£2	£5	£8/£15
1887	R of Victoria struck over V (or I)			---	£20/£30
1887	Proof Gartered Shield		--	---	£50/£75

Being the same size and design as the half-sovereign many were gold plated and passed as such. This led to the withdrawal of this design of sixpence.

1887 Pattern - Gartered Shield - date above crown

Reverse --B-- CROWNED VALUE IN WREATH:

Date	Mintage	Fine	V.F.	E.F.	abt. Unc/FDC
1887	Included above	£1	£2	£4	£8/£12
1887	Proof Crowned Value In Wreath			---	£60/£90
1887	Patterns by Spink, Lion-Shield-Unicorn Reverse: in gold, brass, copper, tin and aluminium.				
1888	4,197,698	£1	£3	£10	£16/£25
1888	A proof	---	---	---	£115
1889	8,738,928	£1	£3	£10	£20/£30
1890	9,386,955	£1	£4	£14	£28/£42
1890	A proof	---	---	---	£115
1891	7,022,734	£1	£3	£12	£24/£30
1892	6,245,746	£1	£3	£10	£20/£30
1893	7,350,619 Jub. Hd.	£65	£175	£550	£800/£1500
1893	(KB Coins '94)	"Extr. rare gdVF" £425			---/---

OLD or WIDOW HEAD

Date	Mintage	Fine	V.F.	E.F.	abt. Unc/FDC
1893	Included above	£1	£4	£12	£20/£30
1893	A proof	---	---	£25	£50/£75
1894	3,467,704	£1	£5	£16	£30/£40
1895	7,024,631	£1	£5	£15	£30/£40
1896	6,651,699	£1	£5	£15	£30/£40
1897	5,031,498	£1	£5	£15	£30/£40
1898	5,914,100	£1	£5	£16	£30/£45
1899	7,996,804	£1	£5	£15	£30/£40
1900	8,984,354	£1	£5	£12	£20/£30
1901	5,108,757	£1	£5	£12	£20/£30

The sixpence became known as a "TANNER". The cab fare from the City of London to Tanner's Hill cost sixpence. "A Tanner One"

SIXPENCES

19mm Silver .925

Date	Mintage	Fine	V.F.	E.F.	abt. Unc/FDC
EDWARD VII		CROWNED SIXPENCE WITHIN WREATH			
1902	6,367,378	£1	£2	£8	£10/£18
1902	15,123 proofs with matt finish	--	--	---	FDC £20
1903	5,410,096	£1	£5	£15	£40/£60
1904	4,487,098	£2	£8	£25	£60/£85
1904	(noted 1996)	"Toned UNC"		---	£80
1905	4,235,556	£2	£8	£22	£50/£70
1906	7,641,146	£1	£3	£14	£30/£40
1906	(noted 1996)	--	--	"FDC"	---/£35
1907	8,733,673	£1	£4	£16	£30/£45
1908	6,739,491	£1	£7	£21	£45/£65
1909	6,584,017	£1	£4	£15	£35/£50
1910	12,490,724	£1	£4	£9	£12/£25
1910	(noted 1996)	--	--	"BU.FDC"	---/£25

MODIFIED EFFIGY : in the absence of a direct comparison, the modified effigy (or modified head) can be distinguished by the initials which appear on the truncation of the neck. Before modification, the initials B.M. are placed near the centre of truncation. After modification they appear, ***without stops***, well to the right thus: BM (not B.M.) The initials are those of the designer of the coin: Bertram Mackennal.

19mm Silver .925 until 1920, then .500

Date	Mintage	Fine	V.F.	E.F.	abt. Unc/FDC
GEORGE V	LION ON CROWN				
1911	9,155,310	---	£1.50	£7	£10/£15
1911	(noted 1996)		"Unc. Nice tone"		---/£14
1911	6,007 proofs	---	---	---	£22/£30
1911	(noted 1996) proof	---	---	"FDC"	---/£35
1912	10,984,129	---	£2	£12	£24/£36
1913	7,499,833	---	£3	£12	£24/£36
1914	22,714,602	---	£1	£5	£9/£15
1915	15,694,597	---	£1	£5	£9/£15
1916	22,207,178	---	£1	£5	£9/£15
1917	7,725,475	---	£2	£12	£24/£36
1918	27,558,743	---	£1	£6	£10/£15
1919	13,375,447	---	£1	£8	£18/£25
1920	14,136,287:				
1920	Silver .925	---	£2	£9	£18/---
1920	Silver .500	---	£1.50	£8	£15/£24
1921	30,339,741	---	£1	£6	£12/£24
1921	(noted 1996)	---	---	Nice.BU"	---/£20
1922	16,878,890	---	£1	£7	£15/£24
1923	6,382,793	---	£3	£15	£25/£40
1924	17,444,218	---	£1	£5	£10/£15
1925	12,720,558	---	£1	£6	£12/£20
1925	With new broader rim		£1.50	£9	£18/£25
1925	A pattern of the 1928 design in nickel				---
1926	21,809,261	---	£1	£9	£16/£25
1926	Modified Effigy (page 23)	£1	£3	£8	£12/£18
1927	68,939,873	£1	£2	£5	£9/£15
1927	15,000 proofs - Rev. new OAK/ACORN design				£12/£20
1928	23,123,384	---	50p	£5	£9/£12
1929	28,319,326	---	50p	£3	£5/ £9
1930	16,990,289	---	60p	£3	£7/£10
1931	16,873,268 ★	---	£1	£4	£7/£12
1931	A proof	---	---	---	£175
1932	9,406,117 ★	---	£1	£6	£15/£25
1933	22,185,083	---	50p	£3	£5/ £8
1933	A proof	---	---	---	£180
1934	9,304,009	---	60p	£4	£7/£12
1935	13,995,621	---	50p	£3	£5/ £7
1936	24,380,171	---	50p	£3	£5/ £7

★ these have a finer grained (milled) edge

SIXPENCES

EDWARD VIII (Duke of Windsor)

SIX LINKED RINGS of ST. EDWARD

1937	(noted 1989)	---	---	"abt.FDC"	£9,500
1937	(noted 1996)	---	---	"abt.FDC"	£11,000

Date	Mintage	Fine	V.F.	E.F.	Unc/abt. FDC
GEORGE VI	*50% SILVER, 50% ALLOY to 1946 - 19mm*				
1937	22,302,524	---	25p	£1.50	£3/ £5
1937	26,402 proofs	---	---	---	£3/ £5
1938	13,402,701	---	---	£3	£6/£12
1939	28,670,304	---	---	£1	£3/ £4
1940	20,875,196	---	---	£1	£3/ £4
1941	23,186,616	---	---	£1	£2/ £3
1942	44,942,785	---	---	£1	£3/ £4
1943	46,927,111	---	---	£1	£3/ £4
1944	37,952,600	---	---	£1	£2/ £3
1945	39,939,259	---	---	£1	£2/ £3
1946	43,466,407	---	---	£1	£2/ £3
	CUPRO-NICKEL				
1946	Proof, for new coinage, in cupro-nickel			---	/£400
1947	29,993,263	---	---	50p	£1/ £3
1948	88,323,540	---	---	50p	£1/ £3

Monogram GRI was changed to GRVI in 1949 when title IND: IMP: (INDAE IMPERATOR) - Emperor of India- was relinquished

Date	Mintage	Fine	V.F.	E.F.	Unc/abt. FDC
1949	41,355,515	---	---	75p	£2/ £4
1950	32,741,955	---	---	75p	£2/ £6
1950	17,513 proofs	---	---	---	£4/ £6
1951	40,399,491	---	---	65p	£2/ £5
1951	20,000 proofs	---	---	---	£4/ £6
1952	1,013,477	50p	£2	£12	£25/£40

Date	Mintage	Fine	V.F.	E.F.	abt. Unc/FDC
ELIZABETH II	NATIONAL EMBLEMS INTERTWINED				
1953	70,323,876	---	---	25p	65p/£1.50
1953	40,000 proofs	---	---	---	£2/ £4
	BRITT: OMN: discontinued				
1954	105,241,150	---	---	35p	£2/ £4
1955	109,929,554	---	---	20p	£1/ £2
1956	109,841,555	---	---	20p	£1/ £2
1957	105,654,290	---	---	20p	£1/ £2
1958	123,518,527	---	---	65p	£2/ £3
1959	93,089,441	---	---	---	£1/ £2
1960	103,288,346	---	---	50p	£2/ £5
1961	115,052,017	---	---	50p	£2/ £5
1962	178,359,637	---	---	---	50p/ £1
1963	112,964,000	---	---	---	50p/ £1
1964	152,336,000	---	---	---	50p/ £1
1965	129,644,000	---	---	---	20p/50p
1966	175,696,000	---	---	---	20p/50p
1966	"Mule" with Commonwealth Portrait @ auction 1993				£396
1967	240,788,000	---	---	---	15p/45p
1970	750,476 proofs for LAST STERLING set				£1/ £3

Various 'pointings' have been noted:

1953 ELIZABETH - ELIZABETH

1955 SIXPENCE - SIXPENCE

1964 and 1965 REGINA - REGINA

Letters point *TO* or *BETWEEN* rim beads

Date			V.F.	E.F.	abt. Unc./FDC
GEORGE V		ESC refers to Seaby's "The English Silver Coinage"			
PATTERNS by HUTH		Central Star bears LEGS OF MAN			
1913	ESC 1481A	Pattern for eightpence in copper			- - -
	ESC 1481	OCTORINO	- - -	- - -	£350/ - - - -
	ESC 1481	Noted (Seaby 1990) abt.FDC			£450
1913	ESC 1482	EIGHTPENCE in silver		- - -	- - - - / £450
	ESC 1482A	EIGHT PENCE in copper		- - -	- - - -
		(Spink 1980) in iron			£225/ - - - -

These items appear only very rarely.

TENPENCES

Date		V.F.	E.F.	abt. Unc./FDC
VICTORIA One Franc				Silver 23mm
1867	Pattern - ESC 1416 ONE FRANC/TEN PENCE	£400		£800/£1200

Briefly: specially struck silver coins are distributed to as many old men and women as the Monarch has years; those years being 'expressed' in pence. Thus, on the Monarch's fortieth birthday, 40 men and 40 women each receive 40 pence or four Maundy sets at tenpence per set. The following year the distribution would be to 41 men and 41 women: four sets plus an extra penny. There are additonal sums, paid in conventional notes and coins, in lieu of food and clothing. The distribution takes place on Maundy Thursday: the day before Good Friday.

MAUNDY SETS

SILVER

FACE VALUE TEN PENCE THE SET OF FOUR COINS

GEORGE IV

Date		V.F.	E.F.	abt. Unc./FDC
1822		£30	£65	£120/£150
1822	A proof set (ESC 2426)	---	---	£150
1823		£25	£60	£100/£125
1824		£30	£80	£125/£140
1825		£25	£60	£100/£125
1826		£25	£60	£100/£125
1827		£25	£60	£100/£125
1828		£25	£60	£100/£125
1828	A proof set (ESC 2433)	---	---	£150
1829		£25	£60	£100/£125
1830		£25	£60	£100/£125

WILLIAM IV

Silver as illustrated

Date	VF.	EF.	abt. FDC from/to
1831	£35	£80	£150/£200
1831	Proof		£100/£250
1831	Proof in gold		----
1832	£35	£80	£120/£150
1833	£35	£80	£120/£150
1834	£35	£80	£130/£200
1835	£35	£80	£120/£150
1836	£35	£80	£120/£150
1837	£35	£80	£120/£150

VICTORIA MAUNDY SETS

Young Head

Date	Sets	EF.	abt Unc/FDC
1838	4,158	£35	£55/£70
1838	Proofs	---	£115
1838	Proofs in gold		---
1839	4,125	£35	£50/£70
1839	Proofs	---	£185
1840	4,125	£35	£50/£65
1841	2,574	£35	£50/£65
1842	4,125	£35	£50/£65
1843	4,158	£35	£50/£65
1844	4,158	£35	£50/£65
1845	4,158	£35	£50/£65
1846	4,158	£35	£50/£65
1847	4,158	£35	£55/£70
1848	4,158	£35	£50/£65
1849	4,158	£42	£60/£75
1850	4,158	£35	£55/£70
1851	4,158	£35	£55/£70
1852	4,158	£35	£55/£70
1853	4,158	£35	£55/£70
1853	Proofs	---	£350/£500
1854	4,158	£36	£50/£65
1855	4,158	£36	£50/£65
1856	4,158	£36	£50/£65
1857	4,158	£36	£55/£70
1858	4,158	£36	£55/£70
1859	4,158	£36	£55/£70
1860	4,158	£36	£50/£65
1861	4,158	£36	£50/£65
1862	4,158	£36	£50/£65
1863	4,158	£36	£50/£65
1864	4,158	£36	£50/£65
1865	4,158	£36	£50/£65
1867	4,158	£36	£50/£65
1867	Proofs		£265
1868	4,158	£36	£50/£65
1869	4,158	£36	£50/£65
1870	4,488	£36	£50/£65
1871	4,488	£36	£50/£65
1871	Proof Auct.89		£410

Young Head

Date	Sets	EF.	abt Unc/FDC
1872	4,328	£36	£50/£65
1873	4,162	£36	£50/£65
1874	4,488	£36	£50/£65
1875	4,154	£36	£50/£65
1876	4,488	£36	£50/£65
1877	4,488	£36	£50/£65
1878	4,488	£36	£50/£65
1878	Proofs	£50	£200
1879	4,488	£36	£50/£65
1880	4,488	£36	£50/£65
1881	Proofs	---	£200
1882	4,488	£36	£50/£65
1883	4,488	£36	£50/£65
1884	4,488	£36	£50/£65
1885	4,488	£36	£50/£65
1886	4,488	£36	£50/£65
1887	4,488	£40	£55/£75

Jubilee Head

Date	Sets	EF.	abt Unc/FDC
1888	4,488	£36	£50/£65
1888	Proofs	---	---
1889	4,488	£45	£55/£70
1890	4,488	£45	£55/£70
1891	4,488	£45	£55/£70
1892	4,488	£45	£55/£70

Old or Widow Head

Date	Sets	EF.	abt Unc/FDC
1893	8,976	£25	£35/£45
1894	8,976	£25	£35/£45
1895	8,877	£25	£35/£45
1896	8,476	£25	£35/£45
1897	8,976	£20	£30/£40
1898	8,976	£25	£35/£45
1898★	(1994)	"FDC orig. case"	£58
1899	8,976	£25	£35/£45
1900	8,976	£25	£35/£45
1901	8,976	£25	£35/£45

Original Documentation Adds Value. Add £6/£9 for contemporary dated case.
1898★ No 'official' case but there were cases "of the time" by various institutions.

EDWARD VII

Date	Sets	EF.	F.D.C. from/to
1902	8,976	£30	£35/£50
1902	15,123	matt	proofs £40
1903	8,976	£30	£35/£45
1904	8,876	£30	£35/£45
1905	8,976	£30	£35/£45
1906	8,800	£30	£35/£40
1906	Dated	octagonal	case £5
1907	8,760	£30	£35/£40
1908	8,760	£30	£35/£40
1909	1,983	£35	£45/£55
1910	1,440	£40	£50/£60

GEORGE V

Date	Sets	EF.	Unc/FDC
1911	1,768	£30	£40/£45
1911	proofs	---	£60
1912	1,246	£25	£35/£40
1913	1,228	£25	£35/£40
1914	982	£42	£50/£60
1915	1,293	£25	£35/£40
1916	1,128	£25	£35/£40
1917	1,237	£25	£35/£40
1918	1,375	£25	£35/£40
1919	1,258	£25	£35/£40
1920	1,399	£25	£35/£40
1921	1,386	£25	£35/£40
1922	1,373	£75	£100/£150
1923	1,430	£35	£45/£60
1924	1,515	£25	£35/£45
1925	1,438	£25	£35/£45
1926	1,504	£25	£35/£45
1927	1,647	£25	£35/£45
1928	1,642	£25	£35/£45
1929	1,761	£25	£35/£45
1930	1,724	£25	£35/£45
1931	1,759	£25	£35/£45
1932	1,835	£25	£35/£45
1933	1,872	£25	£35/£45
1934	1,887	£25	£35/£45
1935	1,928	£30	£45/£55
1936	1,323	£35	£50/£60

Orig. Documents Add Value

MAUNDY ODDMENTS (Virtually Mintlike)

	1d	2d	3d	4d
1822	£10	£22	£25	£30
1822	3d has small head			
1850	£6	--	--	£6
1870	£5	--	--	--
1880	£5	--	--	--
1888	£5	--	--	--
1890	--	--	--	£6
1891	--	£5	--	--
1896	--	£4	--	£6
1898	--	--	--	£7
1900	--	£4	--	--
1902	--	£4	£12	--
1903	£9	£10	--	---
1904	£9	£5	£9	£6
1905	£9	£9	£9	---
1911	--	--	--	£9
1912	£12	£9	£12	£12
1917	£12	£12	--	---
1951	---	---	£15	---
1953	£60	£50	£50	£50

GEORGE VI

Date	Sets	abt Unc/FDC
1937	1,325	£30/£40
1938	1,275	£30/£40
1939	1,234	£30/£40
1940	1,277	£30/£40
1941	1,253	£30/£40
1942	1,231	£30/£40
1943	1,239	£30/£40
1944	1,259	£30/£40
1945	1,355	£30/£40
1946	1,365	£30/£40
1947	1,375	£30/£40
1948	1,385	£30/£40
1949	1,395	£30/£40
1950	1,405	£30/£40
1951	1,468	£30/£40
1952	1,012	£40/£50

1937 to 1946 .500 silver was used.
1947 to 1952 a return to Sterling silver
1949 to 1952 a change of inscription
1952 Maundy was distributed by Queen Elizabeth.
1954 to 1970 a change of inscription.

ELIZABETH II

Date	Complete Sets		Unc/FDC
1953	1,025	St.Paul's Cathedral	£195/£225
1953	In gold	--- (1985)	£5,750
1954	1,020	Westminster Abbey	£35/£45
1955	1,036	Southwark Cathedral	£35/£45
1956	1,088	Westminster Abbey	£35/£45
1957	1,094	St.Alban's Cathedral	£35/£45
1958	1,100	Westminster Abbey	£40/£50
1959	1,106	Windsor	£40/£50
1960	1,112	Westminster Abbey	£40/£50
1961	1,118	Rochester Cathedral	£40/£50
1962	1,125	Westminster Abbey	£40/£50
1963	1,131	Chelmsford	£40/£50
1964	1,137	Westminster	£40/£50
1965	1,143	Canterbury	£40/£50
1966	1,206	Westminster	£40/£50
1967	986	Durham	£40/£50
1968	964	Westminster	£40/£50
1969	1,002	Selby	£40/£50
1970	980	Westminster	£40/£50
1971	1,018	Tewkesbury Abbey	£40/£50
1972	1,026	York Minster	£45/£55
1973	1,004	Westminster	£45/£55
1974	1,042	Salisbury	£45/£55

MAUNDY SETS

Date	Complete Sets			F.D.C. From/ To
ELIZABETH II				
1975	1,050	Peterborough		£45/£55
1976	1,158	Hereford		£45/£55
1977	1,138	Westminster		£45/£55
1978	1,178	Carlisle		£40/£50
1979	1,189	Winchester		£40/£50
1980	1,198	Worcester		£40/£50
1981	1,208	Westminster		£40/£50
1982	1,218	St.David's Cathedral		£40/£50
1983	1,218	Exeter Cathedral		£40/£50
1984	1,243	Southwell Minster		£40/£50
1985	1,248	Ripon Cathedral		£40/£50
1986	1,378	Chichester Cathedral		£50/£60
1987	1,390	Ely Cathedral		£50/£60
1988	1,402	Lichfield Cathedral		£50/£60
1989	1,353	Birmingham Cathedral	(63p)	£50/£60
1990	1,523	St. Nicholas Newcastle	(64p)	£50/£60
1991	1,384	Westminster	(65p)	£50/£60
1992		Chester	(66p)	£50/£60
1993		Wells Cathedral	(67p)	£75/£85
1994		Truro Cathedral	(68p)	
1995		Coventry Cathedral	(69p)	
1996		Norwich Cathedral	(70p)	
1997			(71p)	

Averages of Maundy Sets are influenced by V.A.T.
Thus: a set was reported as 'at auction' £65
Investigation showed £65 + Buyer's Premium of 10%, + VAT on the whole - a total of £82.23

SHILLINGS

GEORGE IV Laureate Head to 1925; Bare Head from L.o.C.
Rev. SHIELD:
Gnd = Garnished, Gtd = Gartered. 23mm L.o.C. = Lion on Crown

Date	Mintage/etc		Fine	V.F.	E.F.	abt Unc/FDC
1820	Pattern	Gnd	(rarity 5)		(1986)	£2,012
1821	2,463,120	Gnd	£5	£15	£50	£75/£125
1821	A proof	Gnd	---	---	---	£400/£600
1823	693,000	Gtd	£15	£50	£125	£225/£350
1823	Noted 1994	(KB Coins)		"FDC toned"		£425
1823	A proof	Gtd	---	---	---	£800
1824	4,158,000	Gtd	£5	£15	£55	£75/£130
1825	2,459,160	Gtd	£5	£20	£60	£95/£150
1825	(Welsh 1996)		--	"Nice BU extremely rare"		£175
1825	5 struck over 3	Gtd		---	---	----
1825	LION on CROWN rev.		£4	£8	£30	£60/£90
1826	6,351,840	L.o.C.	£4	£8	£30	£65/£95
1826	6 struck over a 2nd 2	L.o.C.		£20	£60	£120/£18
1826	A proof	L.o.C.	(ESC 1258)		£95	FDC £200
1827	574,200	L.o.C.	£6	£30	£90	£180/£250
1829	879,120	L.o.C.	£6	£18	£60	£125/£180

WILLIAM IV

Date	Mintage	Fair / Fine	V.F.	E.F.	Unc/ abt FDC
1831	Proofs, plain edge, from set			£135	£300/£400
1834	3,223,440 grained edge	£3	£15	£65	£120/£185
1834	A proof with flat topped '3'		(1988)	"FDC"	£600
1835	1,449,360	£5	£15	£65	£125/£190
1836	3,567,960	£5	£15	£60	£120/£175
1837	479,160	£6	£25	£80	£160/£250
1837	A proof (1984 "abt.FDC" £300) (1996 "abt.FDC" £600)				

VICTORIA

Date	Mintage	Fair / Fine	V.F.	E.F.	Unc/ abt FDC
1838 W.W.	1,956,240 1st Head	£4	£12	£40	£80/£120
1838 W.W.	Proofs	---	---	---	£300/£400
1839 W.W.	5,666,760	£4	£12	£40	£80/£120
1839	Proof (with W.W) from the sets			2nd Head	£350
1839	No W.W. at neck	£2	£12	£45	£90/£150
1839	Proof (no W.W.) grained edge			---	£750
1840	1,639,440	£3 / £9	£25	£85	£125/£200
1841	875,160	£3 / £9	£25	£85	£125/£200
1842	2,094,840	£6	£12	£40	£80/£120
1843	1,465,200	£5	£20	£60	£120/£180
1844	4,466,880	£3	£15	£50	£100/£150
1845	4,082,760	£3	£14	£35	£70/£100
1846	4,031,280	£3	£14	£35	£70/£100
1848 (*)	1,041,480	£20	£62	£200	£300/ ---
1849	645,480	£3	£15	£50	£95/£150
1850	685,080	£90	£300	£925	£1,500
1850	50 over 49	---	---	£1500	/ ---
1851	470,071	£15 / £30	£75	£250	£450/ ---
1851	(J. Welsh 1996)	--	£50	"gdVF rare"	----/ ---
1852	1,306,574	£3	£15	£50	£95/£140
1853	4,256,188	£3	£15	£50	£95/£140
1853	Proofs from the sets		---	---	£300/£500

(*) 1848 all 8 struck over 6

VICTORIA

Date	Mintage	Fine	V.F.	E.F.	Unc/ abt. FDC
1854	552,414	£35	£100	£275	£400/ ---
1855	1,368,499	£3	£15	£45	£85/£115
1856	3,168,000	£3	£15	£45	£85/£115
1857	2,562,120	£3	£15	£45	£85/£115
1857	REG F: Ɔ: (error inverted G)			£165	---/----
1858	3,108,600	£3	£15	£45	£85/£125
1858/8	(Mason 1994) "Unrecorded over-date abt. EF" £65				
1859	4,561,920	£3	£15	£45	£85/£125
1860	1,671,120	£4	£20	£60	£110/£160
1861	1,382,040	£4	£20	£60	£110/£160
1861	1 over tilted I	(1988 near E.F. £45)			---
1862	954,360	£6	£40	£90	£150/£225
1863	859,320	£6	£40	£100	£200/£295

THE FOLLOWING HAVE A DIE NUMBER (above date)

Date	Mintage	Fine	V.F.	E.F.	Unc/ abt. FDC
1864	4,518,360	£3	£15	£45	£85/£120
1865	5,619,240	£3	£15	£45	£85/£120
----	(ESC 1398) Undated pattern (Seaby 1988) "abt.FDC" £650				
1866	4,989,600	£3	£15	£45	£80/£125
1866	(Weeks 1994) "Gem, BU/FDC proof-like"				£125
1866	BBITANNIAR error (Coin Mkt. Values 1995)				"EF" £350
1867	2,166,120	£3	£15	£45	£80/£125
1867	Proof without Die No.		grained (milled) edge		£500/----
1867	Proof without Die No.		plain edge	---	£1000/----
1867	Large head, lower relief		3rd Head	£200	£275/----
1868	3,330,360	£3	£15	£45	£90/£125
1869	736,560	£4	£18	£50	£100/£150
1870	1,467,471	£4	£20	£60	£100/£150
1871	4,910,010	£3	£12	£35	£65/ £95
1872	8,897,781	£3	£12	£35	£65/ £95
1873	6,489,598	£3	£12	£40	£70/£100
1874	5,503,747	£3	£12	£40	£70/£100
1875	4,353,983	£3	£10	£30	£60/ £80
1876	1,057,487	£3	£12	£40	£90/£125
1877	2,980,703	£3	£10	£30	£50/ £75
1877	Believed to exist without Die Number				---/----
1878	3,127,131	£3	£12	£35	£65/ £95
1879	3,611,507	£6	£20	£70	£120/£190
1879	6 over 8 (Die 13)		(Numis. Circ.)		May, 1983

VICTORIA Young Head — DIE NUMBER DISCONTINUED

Reverse: CROWNED ONE SHILLING IN WREATH

Date	Mintage	Fine	V.F.	E.F.	Unc/abt FDC
1879	Fourth Head (Inc. page 29)	£3	£12	£45	£90/---
1880	4,842,786	£2	£7	£25	£50/£75
1881	5,255,332	£2	£7	£25	£50/£75
1881	Shorter line below SHILLING		£7	£25	£50/£75
1882	1,611,786	£9	£25	£80	£150/---
1883	7,281,450	£2	£6	£20	£40/£55
1884	3,923,993	£2	£7	£20	£30/£45
1885	3,336,527	£2	£7	£25	£40/£60
1886	2,086,819	£1	£5	£14	£35/£50
1887	4,034,133 Young head	£3	£12	£36	£50/£86

Jubilee Head — Reverse: SHEILD IN GARTER

Date	Mintage	Fine	V.F.	E.F.	Unc/abt FDC
1887	Included above	£1	£3	£6	£12/£18
1887	1,084 proofs from the sets			---	£50/£75
1888	Last 8 over 7	£4	---	£20	---
1888	4,526,856	£2	£5	£15	£25/£40
1889	7,039,628 but *	£12	£45	£200	£365/---
1889	* Larger head	£2	£4	£15	£30/£60
1890	8,794,042	£2	£4	£20	£40/£60
1891	5,665,348	£2	£4	£20	£35/£55
1892	4,591,622	£2	£4	£22	£40/£60

Proofs exist for other dates but are rarely offered.
Messrs. Seaby's "The English Silver Coinage" lists some 40 patterns.

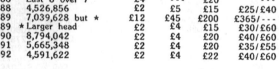

1887 "shuttlecock" varieties : embellishment divides date · 18 ❦ 87
The device points to a rim tooth = Reverse A — Rare
The device points between two teeth = Reverse B — Common

VICTORIA Old, Veiled or Widow Head

THREE SHIELDS within GARTER

Date	Mintage	Fair/Fine	V.F.	E.F.	Unc/abt. FDC
1893	7,039,074	£2	£3	£9	£25/£45
1893	Obv. small letters	--	£6	£18	£40/£60
1893	(noted 1995)	--	--	---	FDC £68
1893	1,312 proofs from the sets				£45/£65
1894	5,953,152	£2	£4	£16	£35/£50
1895	8,880,651	£2	£4	£16	£30/£45
1896	9,264,551	£2	£4	£16	£25/£40
1897	6,270,364	£2	£4	£16	£22/£38
1898	9,768,703	£2	£4	£16	£25/£40
1899	10,965,382	£2	£4	£16	£20/£32
1900	10,937,590	£2	£3	£10	£18/£30
1901	3,426,294	£2/£3	£5	£18	£30/£45

EDWARD VII

Reverse: LION on CROWN

Date	Mintage	Fair/Fine	V.F.	E.F.	Unc/abt. FDC
1902	7,809,481	£1	£4	£12	£18/£30
1902	Noted (Messrs Weeks 1989 Toned Gem Unc £23)				
1902	15,123 proofs matt finish			£5	£15/£25
1903	2,061,823	£3	£9	£35	£60/£95
1904	2,040,161	£3	£9	£40	£60/£95
1905 (*)	488,390	£18/£25	£75	£250	£500/---
1906	10,791,025	£1	£3	£18	£30/£50
1907	14,083,418	£1	£3	£12	£30/£50
1908	3,806,969	£2	£9	£40	£60/£95
1909	5,664,982	£2	£5	£40	£60/£100
1910	26,547,236	£1	£3	£12	£20/£30

(*) Such a rarity attracts the forger !!

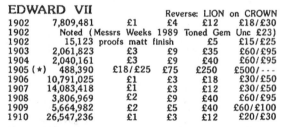

GEORGE V

Reverse: Lion-on-Crown · Date Divided · Inner Circle

Date	Mintage	Fine	V.F.	E.F.	Unc/abt FDC
1911	20,065,901	£1	£2	£8	£16/£24
1911	6,007 proofs		---	---	£28/£35
1912	15,594,009	---	£3	£18	£30/£50
1913	9,011,509	£2	£5	£26	£45/£70
1913	(noted 1996)	---	--	"BU"	---/£60
1913	(noted 1996)	---	--	"FDC"	---/£75
1914	23,415,843	---	£2	£6	£10/£16
1915	39,279,024	---	£2	£4	£9/£14
1916	35,862,015	---	£2	£5	£10/£16
1917	22,202,608	---	£2	£6	£12/£18
1918	34,915,934	---	£2	£6	£10/£16
1919	10,823,824	---	£2	£9	£20/£30

SILVER REDUCED to .500

Date	Mintage	Fine	V.F.	E.F.	Unc/abt FDC
1920	22,825,142	---	£2	£9	£20/£30
1921	22,648,763	---	£3	£18	£30/£50
1921	(noted 1996) "BU Gem raee, exceptional strike"				---/£60
1922	27,215,738	---	£2	£10	£20/£30
1923	14,575,243	---	£2	£10	£20/£30
1923	Trial Piece in nickel		---	£200	£400
1924	Trial in nickel	---	---	£200	£400
1924	9,250,095	45p	£2.50	£12	£18/£35
1925	A pattern in nickel		---	---	
1925	Pattern in lead - obverse worded MODEL -"nr.VF" £175 (1990)				
1925	5,418,764	£1	£5	£20	£36/£62
1926	22,516,453	45p	£2.50	£12	£20/£36
1926	Modified Effigy	---	£2.50	£8	£20/£32
1927	9,262,344	---	£2.50	£8	£22/£32

Obverse 1 = above B.M. the neck is hollow. Reverse A = GEORGIVS (I TWIXT beads)

Obverse 2 = above B.M. the neck is flat. Reverse B = GEORGIVS (I points TO bead)

1911 Varieties : 1 + A; 1 + B; 2 + A; 2 + B.
1912 Varieties : IMP closely spaced; I M P widely spaced.
1920 Varieties : Obverse 1; Obverse 2.

GEORGE V

Reverse:Lion-on-Crown · Date at right · No inner circle

Date	Mintage	Fine	V.F.	E.F.	abt. Unc/FDC
1927	NEW DESIGN	---	£2	£9	£18/£25
1927	15,000 proofs	---	---	---	£18/£25
1928	18,136,778	---	£1	£5	£10/£15
1929	19,343,006	---	£1	£5	£10/£15
1930	3,137,092	---	£6	£20	£40/£60
1931	6,993,926	---	£1	£6	£12/£20
1932	12,168,101	---	£1	£5	£10/£15
1933	11,511,624		£1	£6	£12/£20
1933	(noted 1996)		--	"FDC"	£35
1934	6,138,463	---	£2	£10	£20/£30
1935	9,183,462	---	£1	£5	£10/£15
1936	11,910,613	---	£1	£5	£10/£15

Bullion Value only

EDWARD VIII (Duke of Windsor)

Reverse: LION SEJANT GUARDANT (see page 32)

1936 a few "Scottish" but no "English" "Guesstimate" £12,000

GEORGE VI

50% SILVER/50% ALLOY until 1947

Date	Mintage	Fine	V.F.	E.F.	abt. Unc/FDC
1937E	8,359,122	---	---	£2	£5/£6
1937E	26,402 proofs	---	---	---	£8
1937S	6,748,875	---	---	£2	£4/£5
1937S	26,402 proofs	-	---	---	£5/£8
1938E	4,833,436	---	---	£4	£15/£20
1938S	4,797,852	---	---	£4	£15/£20
1939E	11,052,677	---	---	£1	£4/£6
1939S	10,263,892	---	---	£1	£4/£6
1940E	11,099,126	---	---	£1	£4/£6
1940S	9,913,089	---	---	£1	£4/£6
1941E	11,391,883	---	---	£1	£4/£6
1941S	8,086,030	---	---	£2	£5/£7
1942E	17,453,643	---	---	£1	£3/£4
1942S	13,676,759	---	---	£1	£3/£4
1943E	11,404,213	---	---	£1	£3/£4
1943S	9,824,214	---	---	£1	£3/£4
1944E	11,586,752	---	---	£1	£3/£4
1944S	10,990,167	---	---	£1	£3/£4
1945E	15,143,404	---	---	60p	£2/£4
1945S	15,106,270	---	---	60p	£2/£4
1946E	18,663,797	---	---	50p	£2/£3
1946E	Pattern, proof, or trial in cupro-nickel			---	----
1946S	16,381,501	---	---	50p	£2/£3
1947E	12,120,611	---	---	75p	£3/£4
1947S	12,282,223	---	---	£1	£4/£6
1948E	45,576,923	---	---	£1	£3/£6
1948S	45,351,937	---	---	£1	£3/£6

Bullion Value only

Bullion Value only

Bullion Value only

Bullion Value only

GEORGE VI (continued) — CUPRO-NICKEL 23mm

Date	Mintage	Fine	V.F.	E.F.	Unc. from/to
1949E	19,328,405	---	---	£1	£4/£6
1949S	21,243,074	---	---	£2	£4/£8
1950E	19,243,872	---	---	£1.50	£4/£6
1950E	17,513 proofs	---	---	---	F.D.C £5/£6
1950S	14,299,601	---	---	£2	£5/£7
1950S	17,513 proofs	---	---	---	F.D.C £5/£6
1951E	9,956,930	---	---	£1	£4/£6
1951E	20,000 proofs	---	---	---	F.D.C £6/£7
1951S	10,961,174	---	---	£2	£5/£7
1951S	20,000 proofs	---	---	---	F.D.C £5/£6
1952E	(*) 1 known outside Royal Collection				
1952E	(*) This may be a proof of that date (Coincraft '95)				£8,000

Suffix E = English; and S = Scottish. In 1937 these coins were struck with English, and Scottish, symbols and were circulated, generally, throughout the United Kingdom. The practice continued until 1966; and for 1970.

> Some Heraldic terms:
> RAMPANT - such as lion rampant, see reverse of right-hand 1953,
> STATANT GUARDANT - see left-hand 1937 and 1951 below.
> PASSANT GUARDANT - the three leopards, left-hand 1953.
> SEJANT GUARDANT - sitting, facing: right-hand 1937 and 1951 below.

Passant guardant is sometimes described as couchant (lying down), but the raised paw indicates otherwise. The three leopards are still referred to as such on old coinage, but on modern strikings are likely to be referred to as three lions.

An old 'joke' comes to mind: "Three Leopards lion down".

> 1946E Reverse A İND Reverse B Ï̇ND
> A 'I' points TO a rim bead, B BETWEEN two beads.

ELIZABETH II — CUPRO-NICKEL 23mm

Date	Mintage	Fine	V.F.	E.F.	Unc. from/to
1953E	41,942,894	---	---	30p	£1/ £2
1953	Head both sides, undated but BRITT.OMN				£300
1953E	40,000 proofs	---	---	FDC	£4/ £6
1953S	20,663,528	---	---	30p	£1/ £2
1953S	40,000 proofs	---	---	FDC	£4/ £6
1954E	30,262,032 BRITT. OMN discontinued			45p	£2/ £4
1954S	26,771,735	---	---	36p	£2/ £4
1955E	45,259,908	---	---	36p	£2/ £4
1955S	27,950,906	---	---	50p	£3/ £6
1956E	44,907,008	---	---	£1	£6/£12
1956S	42,853,637	---	---	£1	£6/£12
1957E	42,774,217	---	---	25p	£2/ £4
1957S	17,959,988	---	---	£3	£12/£18
1958E	14,392,305	---	---	£3	£10/£15
1958S	40,822,557	---	---	25p	£1/ £2
1959E	19,442,778	---	---	25p	£1/ £2
1959S	1,012,988	15p	50p	£3	£12/£18
1960E	27,027,914	---	---	25p	£1/ £2
1960S	14,376,932	---	---	25p	£1/ £2
1961E	39,816,907	---	---	15p	£1/ £2
1961S	2,762,558	---	10p	75p	£3/ £6
1961S	A proof	offered in 1984		---	£200
1962E	36,704,379	---	---	---	50p/ £1
1962S	18,967,310	---	---	---	50p/ £1
1963E	44,714,000	---	---	---	50p/ £1
1963S	32,300,000	---	---	---	15p/30p
1964E	8,590,900	---	---	---	30p/50p
1964S	5,239,100	---	---	---	50p/75p
1965E	9,216,000	---	---	---	30p/75p
1965S	2,774,000	---	---	---	50p/ £1
1966E	15,005,000 includes 3,000 minted in 1967				25p/45p
1966S	15,607,000 includes 3,000 minted in 1967				25p/45p
1966S	Head/Tail reversed ↑↓	---	---	---	£30/£50
1968	Decimal equivalent FIVE NEW PENCE introduced				
1970E	750,476 proofs for LAST STERLING set				75p/ £1
1970S	750,476 proofs for LAST STERLING set				75p/ £1

VICTORIA: FLORINS (Two Shillings)

Date		Silver 27 mm		Fine	V.F.	E.F.	abt Unc/FDC
1848		'GODLESS' (having no DEI GRATIA) patterns					£700
1848		As above but with grained (milled) edge					£2350
1849		413,830	'Godless'	£6	£25	£60	$100/£150
		GOTHIC - date appears in Roman - third column - 30mm.					
1851		1,540	mdcccli	£2000 (report 1995)			----/----
1852		1,014,552	mdccclii	£6	£25	£75	£150/£200
1852		ii struck over i	(Messrs. Weeks 1993)			£95	"abtEF"
1853	*	3,919,950	mdcccliii	£6	£30	£95	£175/£300
1853		Proof		----	----	----	£800/£1000
1854		550,413	mdcccliv	£200	£500	£1800	----/----
1855		831,017	mdccclv	£6	£25	£100	£175/£250
1856	*	2,201,760	mdccclvi	£6	£26	£110	£200/£275
1857		1,671,120	mdccclvii	£6	£25	£100	£150/£250
1857		Proof	(ESC815)	----	----	----	£875
1858	+	2,239,380	mdccclviii	£6	£25	£80	£150/£200
1858		(Seaby 1989) "no stop after date"				£110	"EF/gdEF"
1859	+	2,568,060	mdccclvix	£6	£25	£100	£150/£200
1860		1,475,100	mdccclx	£7	£30	£125	£200/£300
1862		594,000	mdccclxii	£20	£100	£300	£400/£600
1863		938,520	mdccclxiii	£40	£150	£500	£950/£1400
1864		1,861,200	mdccclxiv	£6	£25	£100	£175/£250
1865	!	1,580,044	mdccclxv	£6	£30	£105	£175/£225
1865	!	(Mason 1994)				"abt.UNC"	£110/----
1866	!	914,760	mdccclxvi	£6	£30	£125	£180/£250
1867		423,720	mdccclxvii	£15	£60	£200	£340/£450
1868		896,940	mdccclxviii	£6	£30	£125	£180/£250
1869		297,000	mdccclxix	£5	£25	£100	£150/£200
1870		1,080,648	mdccclxx	£5	£25	£100	£150/£200
1871		3,425,605	mdccclxxi	£5	£25	£100	£150/£200
1872		7,199,690	mdccclxxii	£4	£22	£80	£120/£175
1873		5,921,839	mdccclxxiii	£4	£22	£70	£120/£190
1874		1,642,630	mdccclxxiv	£4	£24	£80	£140/£200
1875		1,117,030	mdccclxxv	£5	£25	£100	£150/£200
1876		580,034	mdccclxxvi	£5	£26	£100	£165/----
1877		682,292	mdccclxxvii	£5	£26	£100	£165/----
1877		No WW (48 arcs)		£15	£60	£200	----/----
1877		No WW (42 arcs)		£12	£50	£120	£190/----
1878		1,786,680	mdccclxxviii	£5	£25	£100	£150/£200

* Have varieties with no stop after date. Rarity R2
\+ Have varieties with no stop after date. Rarity R
! With colon after date: 1865 R3; 1866 R2
1867 brit: is normal; proofs/patterns have britt:
1874 has variety 'iv struck over iii'. Rarity R2
1887 normal has 33 arcs; variety 46 arcs. Rarity R
R = rare; R2 = very rare; Seaby/Rayner scale.

Silver 27 mm			Fine	V.F.	E.F.	abt. Unc/FDC
1879	1,512,247	mdccclxxix				
Die No.	48 arcs WW	(ESC849B)	£30	£80	----	----
No Die No.	42 arcs	(ESC 850)	£20	£70	(no WW)	----
No Die No.	48 arcs WW	(ESC 851)	£7	£30	£120	£165/£250
No WW	38 arcs	(ESC 852)	£6	£25	£100	£150/£200
1880	2,167,170	mdccclxxx	£4	£24	£90	£150/£225
1880	(noted 1996)		--	"VF+"	£45	----/----
1881	2,570,337	mdccclxxxi	£4	£22	£75	£150/£225
1881	Broken die	mdccclxxri	£4	£22	£90	£150/£225
1883	3,555,667	mdccclxxxiii	£4	£22	£90	£150/£225
1884	1,447,379	mdccclxxxiv	£4	£22	£90	£150/£225
1885	1,758,210	mdccclxxxv	£4	£22	£90	£150/£225
1886	591,773	mdccclxxxvi	£4	£22	£90	£150/£225
1887	1,776,903	mdccclxxxvii	£7	£30	£130	£225/£300

Those above and at left are inscribed: one tenth of a pound
Proofs exist for many dates; they are rare and rarely offered

Date	Mintage		Fair/Fine	V.F.	E.F.	Unc/abt. FDC.
Jubilee Head						28 mm
1887	Included above		£2	£4	£8	£12/£20
1887	1,084	Jubilee Head proofs			£45	£90/££125
1888	1,541,540		£2	£4	£15	£30/£50
1889	2,973,561		£2/£3	£5	£18	£35/£60
1890	1,684,737		£4	£15	£60	£85/£150
1891	836,438		£9	£35	£95	£130/£200
1892	283,401		£12	£40	£85	£140/£200
Old, Veiled or Widow Head						
1893	1,666,103		£2	£6	£25	£50/£75
1893	1,312	proofs		---	---	---/£125
1894	1,952,842		£3	£8	£30	£50/£75
1895	2,182,968		£3	£8	£28	£45/£70
1896	2,944,416		£3	£8	£28	£45/£70
1897	1,699,921		£2/£3	£6	£30	£45/£70
1898	3,061,343		£3	£6	£25	£45/£70
1899	3,966,953		£2	£5	£25	£40/£60
1900	5,528,630		£2	£5	£25	£40/£60
1901	2,648,870		£2	£5	£25	£40/£60

FLORINS (Two Shillings)

28 mm

Date	Mintage	Fine	V.F.	E.F.	abt. Unc/FDC
EDWARD VII					Britannia standing
1902	2,189,575	£3	£9	£25	£40/£65
1902	(noted 1996)		- -	"BU, Gem"	£45
1902	15,123 matt finished proofs				£40/£50
1903	1,995,298	£4	£12	£55	£80/£120
1904	2,769,932	£5	£15	£60	£100/£150
1905	1,187,596	£14	£45	£160	£300/£460
1906	6,910,128	£3	£10	£40	£80/£120
1907	5,947,895	£3	£12	£60	£90/£140
1908	3,280,010	£5	£18	£80	£140/£200
1909	3,482,289	£4	£18	£80	£140/£200
1910	5,650,713	£2	£9	£35	£60/ £95
GEORGE V					Shields/Sceptres in Quarters
1911	5,951,284	£1	£5	£25	£40/ £60
1911	(noted 1996) "Gem. Unc. Lovely Tone"				£55
1911	6,007 proofs		- - -	£40	£50/ £70
1912	8,571,731	£1	£5	£28	£45/ £75
1913	4,545,278	£1	£5	£30	£60/ £80
1914	21,252,701	£1	£3	£12	£20/ £30
1915	12,367,939	£1	£3	£12	£24/ £36
1915	(noted 1996)	- -	"BU, rare"		£30
1916	21,064,337	£1	£3	£12	£24/ £36
1917	11,181,617	£1	£4	£20	£30/ £50
1918	29,211,792	£1	£3	£10	£20/ £30
1919	9,469,292	£1	£4	£15	£30/ £45
FROM 1920 SILVER REDUCED TO 50%					
1920	15,387,833	£1	£5	£20	£40/ £50
1921	34,863,895	£2	£5	£15	£30/ £45
1922	23,861,044	£2	£5	£15	£30/ £45
1923	21,546,533	£2	£5	£15	£28/ £40
1924	4,582,372	£2	£6	£25	£50/ £75
1925	1,404,136	£5	£15	£75	£135/£210
1925	Uniface pattern in lead (Seaby 1990) "vf+" £225				
1926	5,125,410	£3	£9	£25	£45/ £65
1927	15,000 proofs of new design				£40/ £50
1928	11,087,186	£2	£4	£7	£10/ £15
1929	16,397,279	£2	£4	£7	£10/ £15
1930	5,753,568	£2	£4	£8	£12/ £18
1931	6,556,331	£2	£4	£7	£10/ £18
1932	717,041	£3	£15	£65	£125/£225
1933	8,685,303	£2	£4	£8	£16/ £30
1934	none	- - -	- - -	- - -	- - - / - - -
1935	7,540,546	£2	£4	£7	£10/ £18
1936	9,897,448	£2	£4	£8	£12/ £20

1911	Two obverses (see page 9)
1914	Large rim teeth and small rim teeth
1920	BRİTT and BRİTT (rim pointings)

Date	Mintage	Fine	V.F.	E.F.	Unc/ abt. FDC.
EDWARD VIII	as GEORGE VI but monogram ER				
1937			"Guesstimate"		£10,000/£12,000
GEORGE VI			50/50 silver/alloy until 1947		
1937	13,006,781	- - -	- - -	£2	£4/ £6
1937	26,402 proofs		- - -	- - -	£8/£10
1938	7,909,388	- - -	- - -	£5	£12/£16
1939	20,850,607	- - -	- - -	£3	£5/ £8
1939	Proof	- - -	(Spinks 1986)		/£165
1940	18,700,338	- - -	- - -	£2	£3/ £5
1941	24,451,079	- - -	- - -	£2	£3/ £5
1942	39,895,243	- - -	- - -	£2	£3/ £4
1943	26,711,987	- - -	- - -	£2	£3/ £4
1944	27,560,005	- - -	- - -	£2	£3/ £4
1945	25,858,049	- - -	- - -	£2	£3/ £5
1946	22,910,085	- - -	- - -	£2	£3/ £5
	CUPRO-NICKEL				
1946	Trial Piece for new coinage in cupro-nickel,				- - / - -
1947	22,910,085	- - -	- - -	£1	£2/ £4
1948	67,553,636	- - -	- - -	£1	£2/ £4
1949	28,614,939	- - -	- - -	£2	£4/ £8
1949	Proof	- - -	- - -	- - -	£160/- - -
1950	24,357,490	- - -	- - -	£2	£4/ £8
1950	17,513 proofs		- - -	- - -	£6/£10
1951	27,411,747	- - -	- - -	£2	£5/ £8
1951	20,000 proofs		- - -	- - -	£6/£10

FLORINS (Two Shillings)

Date	Mintage	Fine	V.F.	E.F.	abt. Unc/FDC/FDC
ELIZABETH II			Cupro-nickel		28 mm
1953	11,958,710	---	---	£1	£2/£4
1953	40,000 proofs	---	---	---	£4 / £6/ £7
1954	13,085,422	---	---	£5	£20/£30/£40
1955	25,887,253	---	---	£1	£1 / £3/ £4
1956	47,824,500	---	---	£1	£1 / £3/ £4
1957	33,071,282	---	---	£2	£10/£15/£25
1958	9,564,580	---	---	£1	£6/£12
1958	Proof (1995) "Minor surface marks, otherwise superb"				£95/---
1958	Proof Noted 1993 "V.I.P. proof FDC"				£250
1959	14,080,319	---	---	£2	£10/£15/£30
1960	13,831,782	---	---	50p	£1/£3
1961	37,735,315	---	---	50p	£1/£3
1962	35,147,903	---	---	30p	£1/£3
1963	25,562,000	---	---	20p	£1/£3
1964	16,539,000	---	---	20p	£1/£3
1965	48,163,000	---	---	20p	50p/£2
1966	84,041,000	---	---	20p	50p/£2
1967	22,152,000	---	---	20p	50p/£2
1968	17,566,000 dated 1967. Decimals introduced.				
1970	750,476 proofs for Last Sterling set				£3 / £4/ £5

HALF CROWNS

Date	Mintage	Fine	V.F.	E.F.	abt Unc/FDC
GEORGE IV					Silver 32 mm
1820	Garnished Shield	£7	£30	£95	£180/£275
1821	1,435,104 Rev.1	£7	£30	£95	£180/£290
1821	(*) Rev.2	£7	£60	£300	£400/----
1821	Proof	---	---	£300	£600/£950
1822	Proof (only 2 known)		(1993)	"FDC"	£3,650
1823	2,003,760	£175	£650	£1800	£3,000
1823	Shield in Garter	£9	£35	£120	£250/£375
1823	Pattern	(ESC 652)	(1991)	"FDC"	£4,800
1824	465,696 ?	£14	£60	£180	£260/£350
1824	Bare Head	£500	£750	£2650	----/----
1825	2,258,784	£7	£28	£80	£160/£200
1825	Proofs	(ESC 643; and 644)			/£850
1825	Proof (ESC 645) in Barton's Metal : a sandwich of copper and two skins of gold.				(1984) £1,500
1826	2,189,088	£9	£35	£120	£200/£325
1826	Proofs from the sets		---	£150	----/£700
1828	49,890 ?	£12	£50	£180	£260/£350
1829	508,464	£12	£50	£180	£260/£350
	Proofs except 1828 and 1829; patterns 1820/22/23/24				
	Pattern "Binfield" (ESC 655) (1991) " abt.Unc."				£395/----

(*) 1821 Rev.2 subtle differences, e.g. see shamrock stems

Date	Mintage	Fine	V.F.	E.F.	abt Unc/FDC
WILLIAM IV					Silver 32 mm
1831	Currency	£500	(Coincraft Cat. 1995)		----/----
1831	Proofs from the sets (noted 1994)			£295	"gd.EF"
1834 *	993,168 WW	£15	£60	£240	£400/£650
1834 *	WW in script	£7	£30	£110	£200/£290
1835	281,952	£12	£50	£150	£300/£450
1836	1,588,752	£6	£25	£96	£150/£250
1836	6 struck over 5	£12	£50	£150	£250/£325
1837	150,526	£12	£50	£150	£250/£360
1834 *	proofs for both types of signature			----	£950£1200
1834 *	plain edged proofs --		---	----	£2000/£3000

HALF CROWNS

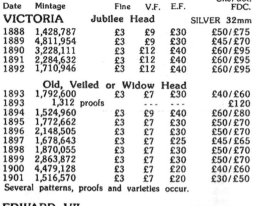

Date	Mintage	Fine	V.F.	E.F.	abt. Unc/FDC.
VICTORIA	**Young Head**				Silver 32 mm
1839a	Raised WW	£250	£650	£2500	----/----
1839a	Proof with grained (milled) edge			----	----/£2500
1839a	Proof with plain edge, from the sets			----	----/ £500
1839b	Proof with two ornamented hair fillets			----	----/£1500
1839c	Proof with two plain hair fillets			----	----/£3500
1839d	Currency, incuse WW	£250	£650	£2500	
1839d	Proof, graine (milled) edge		---	---	----/£3000
1839d	Plain edge proofs, from the sets			---	----/£4500
1840	386,496	£12	£50	£150	£300/£450
1841	42,768	£20	£85	£300	£600/----
1842	486,288	£7	£35	£100	£175/£275
1843	454,608	£16	£60	£200	£300/£450
1844	1,999,008	£6	£25	£90	£150/£240
1845	2,231,856	£6	£25	£90	£150/£240
1846	1,539,668	£6	£25	£90	£150/£240
1848	367,488 8/6	£30	£120	£360	£475/£650
1849	261,360 large date	£10	£50	£175	£250/£360
1849	Smaller date	£12	£55	£200	£275/£375
1850	484,613	£8	£42	£175	£350/----
1853	Proofs from the sets (ESC 687)			---	£1,500
1862	Proofs (ESC 688) and (ESC 689)			---	£2,500
1864	Proof only, for the Albert Memorial			---	£3,000
1874	2,188,599	£4	£20	£80	£160/£225
1875	1,113,483	£4	£22	£75	£145/----
1876	633,221	£4	£24	£80	£150/----
1876	6 struck over 5	---	---	---	----
1877	447,059	£4	£16	£65	£100/£150
1878	1,466,232	£4	£16	£65	£100/£150
1879	901,356	£5	£20	£80	£140/£220
1879	Proof (Seaby 1990)	(ESC704)		"abt.FDC"	£1100
1880	1,346,350	£4	£20	£70	£110/£160
1881	2,301,495	£4	£14	£60	£100/£150
1882	808,227	£4	£25	£75	£125/£200
1883	2,982,779	£4	£16	£60	£120/£200
1884	1,569,175	£4	£20	£65	£120/£200
1885	1,628,438	£4	£20	£65	£120/£200
1886	891,767	£4	£20	£75	£120/£200
1887	261,747 Yng. Head	£4	£22	£75	£120/£200
1887	1,176,299 Jub. Head	£2	£5	£9	£15/£25
1887	1,084 proofs	--	---	---	£125/£145

(a) has one plain, one ornamented hair fillet; WW, on neck, is raised
(b) has two ornamental hair fillets: WW raised
(c) has two plain hair fillets; WW raised
(d) has two plain hair fillets; WW incuse (struck in)

Date	Mintage	Fine	V.F.	E.F.	Unc/abt. FDC.
VICTORIA	**Jubilee Head**				SILVER 32mm
1888	1,428,787	£3	£9	£30	£50/£75
1889	4,811,954	£3	£9	£30	£45/£70
1890	3,228,111	£3	£12	£40	£60/£95
1891	2,284,632	£3	£12	£40	£60/£95
1892	1,710,946	£3	£12	£40	£60/£95
	Old, Veiled or Widow Head				
1893	1,792,600	£3	£7	£30	£40/£60
1893	1,312 proofs		---	---	£120
1894	1,524,960	£3	£9	£40	£60/£80
1895	1,772,662	£3	£7	£30	£50/£70
1896	2,148,505	£3	£7	£30	£50/£70
1897	1,678,643	£3	£7	£25	£45/£65
1898	1,870,055	£3	£7	£30	£50/£70
1899	2,863,872	£3	£7	£30	£50/£70
1900	4,479,128	£3	£7	£20	£40/£60
1901	1,516,570	£3	£7	£20	£30/£50

Several patterns, proofs and varieties occur.

Date	Mintage	Fine	V.F.	E.F.	Unc/abt. FDC.
EDWARD VII					SILVER 32mm
1902	1,316,008	£2	£6	£25	£45/£55
1902	15,123	matt surfaced proofs			£45/£65
1903	274,840	£20	£80	£250	£500/£750
1904	709,652	£12	£50	£200	£400/£600
1904	noted 1995	"Detail sharp and proof-like"			£220/----
1905	166,008	£65	£200	£700	£900/---
1905	(S & B '95)	£150	"Fine/nearly VF"		----/---
1906	2,886,206	£3	£10	£60	£100/£175
1906	(S & B '95)	"nr.UNC, nice tone"		£95	----/---
1907	3,693,930	£3	£10	£60	£120/£180
1908	1,758,889	£4	£15	£80	£160/£225
1909	3,051,592	£3	£12	£75	£125/£200
1910	2,557,685	£3	£10	£50	£90/£140

Proofs noted: 1890 £350; 1864 £825; 1876 £1,250.

GEORGE V

SILVER to 1920; then 50/50 SILVER/ALLOY

Date	Mintage	Fine	V.F.	E.F.	abt. Unc/FDC.
1911	2,914,573	£2	£6	£25	£50/£75
1911	6,007 proofs		---		£60/£70
1912	4,700,789	£3	£9	£30	£55/£85
1913	4,090,160	£3	£10	£40	£80/£120
1914	18,333,003	---	---	£12	£20/£30
1915	32,433,066	£2	£4	£12	£24/£30
1916	29,530,020	£2	£4	£12	£24/£30
1917	11,172,052	£2	£4	£12	£25/£35
1918	29,079,592	£2	£4	£12	£24/£36
1919	10,266,737	£2	£4	£15	£40/£60
	NOW REDUCED TO .500 SILVER				
1920	17,983,077	£1	£2	£20	£40/£60
1921	23,677,889	DEI and DEI	£2	£25	£45/£70
1922	16,396,774	Rev. A	£2	£20	£35/£50
		Rev. B	£3	£25	£40/£60
		Rev.A = Narrow groove twixt crown and shield			
		Rev.B = Wide groove between crown and shield			
1923	26,308,526	£1	£2	£10	£16/£25
1924	5,866,294	£1	£3	£25	£50/£75
1925	1,413,461	£3	£15	£100	£165/£265
1926	4,473,516	£1	£3	£30	£60/£90
1926	No colon after OMN	£5	£25	£165	£260/----
1926	Modified Effigy (page 23)		£4	£30	£55/£80
1927	6,852,872	£1	£3	£15	£30/£45
1927	15,000 proofs, new design			---	£20/£30
1928	18,762,727	£1	£3	£8	£16/£25
1929	17,632,636	£1	£3	£8	£16/£25
1930	809,501	£6	£15	£75	£150/£225
1931	11,264,468	£1	£3	£9	£18/£25
1932	4,793,643	£1	£3	£15	£30/£50
1933	10,311,494	£1	£3	£9	£18/£25
1934	2,422,399	£1	£3	£25	£40/£70
1935	7,022,216	£1	£3	£6	£12/£18
1935	A proof changed hands in 1975 for			---	£160/----
1936	7,039,423	£1	£3	£6	£12/£18

1928 Rosette: ★ = Rev. A; ★ = Rev. B   1929 Varieties as for 1928

EDWARD VIII

(Duke of Windsor) ·500 SILVER

1937 Standard bearing Royal Arms (1993) £16,000/£20,000

GEORGE VI

.500 SILVER until 1947 - 32mm

Date	Mintage	Fine	V.F.	E.F.	Unc/abt FDC
1937	9,106,440	£1	£2	£3	£6/£9
1937	26,402 proofs	--	--	FDC	£10
1938	6,426,478	£1	£2	£5	£15/£20
1938	(noted 1996)	"FDC superb"		--	£25
1939	15,478,635	£1	£2	£3	£6/£9
1940	17,948,439	£1	£2	£3	£6/£9
1941	15,773,984	£1	£2	£3	£6/£9
1942	31,220,090	£1	£2	£3	£6/£9
1943	15,462,875	£1	£2	£3	£6/£9
1944	15,255,165	£1	£2	£3	£6/£9
1945	19,849,242	£1	£2	£3	£5/£8
1946	22,724,873	£1	£2	£3	£5/£8
	NOW CUPRO-NICKEL (no silver)				
1947	21,911,484	--	£1	£2	£4/£6
1948	71,164,703	--	£1	£2	£4/£6
1949 ★	28,272,512	--	£1	£2	£5/£8
1950	28,335,500	--	£1	£2	£5/£7
1950	17,513 proofs	--	--	--	£6/£9
1951	9,003,520	--	£1	£3	£6/£9
1951	20,000 proofs	--	--	--	£5/£8
1952	1 Sold by "Private Treaty" in 1991				£28,500

★ IND: IMP (Emperor of India) discontinued from 1949

HALF CROWNS

Date	Mintage	Fine	V.F.	E.F.	abt. Unc/FDC.
ELIZABETH II		CUPRO-NICKEL 32mm			
1953	4,333,214	--	DEI ..	£1	£2/£3
1953	I points between rim beads DEI			£1	£3/£6
1953	40,000 proofs	--	--	--	£4/£7
1954	11,614,953	--	--	£4	£15/£25
1954	Proof	(1985 £225) (1996 £300)			
1955	23,628,726	--	--	£1	£4/£6
1955	(noted 1996)	--	--	"Nice B.U."	--/£7
1956	33,934,909	--	--	£1	£4/£6
1957	34,200,563	--	--	£1	£3/£5
1958	15,745,668	--	--	£3	£12/£20
1959	9,028,844	--	--	£4	£25/£30
1960	19,929,191	--	--	£1	£3/£4
1961 ★	25,887,897	--	--	--	£1/£2
1962 ★	24,013,312	--	--	--	£1/£2
1963 ★	17,557,600	--	--	--	£1/£2
★	(noted 1996) All seen offered in "BU"				--/£5
1964	5,973,600	--	--	£1	£2/£3
1965	9,878,400	--	--	--	£1/£2
1966	13,384,000	--	--	--	70p/£2
1967	18,895,200	--	--	--	60p/£1
1968	14,163,200 but dated 1967			--	
1969	Halfcrowns were demonetized		31st December.		
1970	Proofs from the 8-coin set			--	£2/£4

(Four Shillings) DOUBLE FLORINS

Date	Mintage		Fine	V.F.	E.F.	abt. Unc/FDC
VICTORIA		Jubilee Head				SILVER 36mm
1887	483,347	Roman I	£5	£10	£20	£30/£45
1887	Roman I proof		--	--	---	£175/£250
1887	Arabic 1 in date		£5	£10	£20	£40/£50
1887	Arabic 1 proof		--	--	---	£175/£225
1888	243,340		£6	£15	£30	£60/£90
1888 ★	Inverted 1 for second I		£10	£30	£60	£120/£180
1889	1,185,111		£5	£10	£20	£40/£60
1889 ★	Inverted 1 for second I		£10	£30	£60	£120/£180
1890	782,146		£6	£12	£25	£50/£75
1890	Pattern with reverse worded DOUBLE FLORIN					---

★ 2nd I of VICTORIA J.E.B. at truncation = Designer/Engraver Joseph Boehm

GEORGE V		SILVER 36mm
1910	Double Florin in gold --- (1986)	£5,700
1911	Rare Plain and grained edge patterns (sundry metals)	
1911	As picture but DOUBLE FLORIN (1989 abtFDC £450)	
1914	With the words TWELVE GROATS and in various metals	
GEORGE VI		SILVER 36mm
1950	Patterns, grained edge, George and Dragon	ext. rare
1950	As previous coin but 'FOUR SHILLINGS' struck into the edge	

SILVER 38mm

Date	Mintage	Fine	V.F.	E.F.	abt. Unc/FDC
GEORGE IV	*Laureate Head · St. George/Dragon Reverse*				
1820	Pattern (ESC 259)	(Dolphin 1993)		"FDC"	£5000
1821	437,976 SECVNDO	£15	£45	£250	£500/£750
1821	(noted 1994)	---	"Virtually FDC"		£750
1821	SECVNDO proof	(noted 1996)		£2500	----/----
1821	Error TERTIO proof	(noted 1996)		----	£4000
1822	124,929 SECVNDO	£20	£60	£350	£700/£1200
1822	SECVNDO proof	---	---	(noted 1996)	£3500
1822	TERTIO	£15	£70	£300	£650/£900
1822	TERTIO proof	---	---	(1986)	£2300
1823	Without edge number, proof only (offers to buy £6000)				
	Bare Head · Shield Reverse				
1825	(ESC 255) BARE HEAD pattern ---			(noted 1996)	£5000
1826	(ESC 257) SEPTIMO proof from the sets			(1987)	£3000
1828	(ESC 263) Pattern in Germanic style			£400 (1983)	-----

Date	Mintage	Fine	V.F.	E.F.	Abt. Unc/FDC
WILLIAM IV					
	MANTLE design as halfcrown Proofs and patterns only				
1831	W.W. (ESC 271)(near FDC, minor defects, Seaby £2750)				
1831	W.W. Proof in gold (Coincraft Cat. 1995)				£60000
1831	W.Wyon (ESC 273)	---	---	£3000	/£4500
1832	Lead Pattern, extreme rarity edge TERTIO			£4000	----
1834	A plain edged proof	---	---	£9000	£11000

Date	Mintage	Fine	V.F.	E.F.	Abt. Unc/FDC
VICTORIA	*YOUNG HEAD*				SILVER 38mm
1837	Incuse Pattern (Auction 1987)				£2600
1837	Pattern, lead, mirror image (Spink 1988)			£650	----
1839	Proofs from the sets (ESC 279)			£1200	£2250/£3250
1844	94,248 Edge VIII : Star-shaped edge stops	£15	£60	£500	£950/£2000
1844	Proof with star-shaped edge stops		---	----	£4000/£7500
1844	Cinquefoil (five leaves) stops		£50	£400	£1200/£1600
1845	159,192 Edge VIII	£15	£60	£400	£750/£1500
1846	Pattern by W.Wyon (ESC 341)	---		(1980)	/£3000
1847	140,976 Edge XI	£20	£75	£500	£1000/£1500
1847	8,000 UNDECIMO proof GOTHIC :	£200	£400	£800	£1500/£2000
1847	(Glendinings '92) "Superb example ..... practically as struck"				£1705
1847	Roy Francis pinpoints Spink-Taisei sale 1988, 1 in gold				£113,000
1847	Error edge SEPTIMO proof GOTHIC			----	-----/-----
1847	Without edge number (ESC 291)			£600	£1200/£1600
1853	460 DECIMO SEPTIMO from the sets			£2000	£3000/£4000
1853	(Whiteaves-Scott '95) "Magnificent Gem FDC"				£4250
1853	Without edge number (ESC 294)			----	£4500/£6000
1879	Return to Young Head. Offers for this exceed				£15,000

"Gothic" crowns have the obverse inscribed, at perimeter thus: mdcccxlvii for 1847, or mdcccliii for 1853

VICTORIA *Jubilee Head* GOLDEN JUBILEE

Date	Mintage		Fine	V.F.	E.F.	abt. Unc/FDC
1887	173,581		£7	£15	£30	£45/ £70
1887	1,084	proofs	--	---	£150	£250/£350
1888	131,899	close date	£10	£30	£60	£90/£140
1888		wider date	£15	£45	£90	£140 £200
1889	1,807,223		£7	£15	£30	£45/ £70
1890	997,862		£10	£25	£60	£90/£140
1891	566,394		£10	£25	£60	£90/£140
1892	451,334		£12	£30	£90	£130 £220

Prices asked often have wide variations, for example: 1887 ABU £30; BU £40; BU Gem £60; FDC £75.

Old, Veiled or Widow Head

Date	Mintage		Fine	V.F.	E.F.	abt. Unc/FDC
1893	1,312	LVI proofs from the sets			£150	£250/£360
1893	497,845	LVI	£7	£30	£50	£95/£145
1893		LVII	£15	£40	£85	£165/£250
1894	144,906	LVII	£6	£30	£95	£175/£250
1894		LVIII	£6	£20	£80	£160/£240
1895	252,862	LVIII	£6	£20	£80	£160/£220
1895		LIX	£6	£20	£80	£160/£220
1896	317,599	LIX	£10	£30	£130	£250/£375
1896		LX	£6	£20	£80	£120/£200
1897	262,118	LX	£6	£20	£30	£120/£200
1897		LXI	£7	£20	£90	£145/£225
1898	161,450	LXI	£15	£40	£95	£180/£275
1898		LXII	£6	£20	£80	£120/£180
1899	166,300	LXII	£6	£20	£80	£120/£180
1899		LXIII	£6	£20	£80	£120/£180
1900	353,356	LXIII	£5	£20	£90	£130/£225
1900		LXIV	£5	£20	£90	£130/£225

EDWARD VII

Date	Mintage	Fine	V.F.	E.F.	abt Unc/FDC
1902	256,020	£20	£40	£60	£110/£125
1902	15,123 proofs with matt surface			£65	£100/£125
1902	(noted 1995)	---	---	"F.D.C."	£177
1902	★ Pattern depicting Edward VII, robed, and on horseback				
1902	Pattern similar to the previous entry, struck in gold				
	★ 1902 Style as Charles I "Tower" (Spinks 1985)				£2,500

GEORGE V *debased silver .500 fineness from 1927*

Date	Mintage	Fine	V.F.	E.F.	abt Unc/FDC
1910	Pattern: flowing interpretation George/Dragon				
1910	Similar but date in exergue reverse (ESC 389)				£3,500
1927	15,030 proofs from the sets			£60	£90/£100
1928	9,034	£30	£60	£90	£125/£175
1928	(J. Welsh 1991)	"Gem BU/FDC"			£150
1929	4,994	£30	£60	£90	£125/£175
1930	4,847	£30	£60	£90	£130/£180
1931	4,056	£35	£70	£140	£180/£290
1932	2,395	£50	£75	£150	£200/£300
1932	4 proofs (noted 1986)			"gdEF/FDC"	£950
1933	7,132	£30	£60	£95	£145/£250
1934	932	£250	£450	£750	£950/£1500
1934	8 proofs (Coincraft Cat. '95)				£4000
1935	714,769 incuse edge lettering		£4	£8	£12/£15
1935	Superior strikings,	---		in special box	£20/£30
1935	2,500 silver proofs, raised edge lettering				£200/£250
1935	A few .925 silver proofs incuse edge lettering				£1750
1935 ★	Some; both incuse and raised, have edge lettering error				
1935	Error edge	£50	£75	£125	£250/£325
1935	30 proofs struck in gold raised edge lettering				£12000
1935	A pattern - date in front of horse's head				----
1936	2,473	£50	£75	£150	£225/£300
1936	3 or 4 proofs are thought to exist			"guesstimate"	£1600

★ correct order of words: DECUS ET TUTAMEN ANNO REGNI

EDWARD VIII *.500 fine silver* 38 mm

1936	Unofficial patterns	---	---	FDC	£20
1936	(noted 1993)	---	---	"abt FDC"	£15
1937	designs similar to George VI			"guesstimate"	£75000

Date	Mintage		Fine	V.F.	E.F.	Abt. Unc/FDC.
GEORGE VI		*.500 fine silver*				38 mm
1937	418,699	Coronation	- - -	£5	£10	£15/£20
1937	26,402	Proofs from the sets			£10	£20/£30
1937	(noted 1996)			"Proof, FDC"		/£35
1937		Proofs with special frosting (V.I.P.) 0.925 silver				£100/£150
1937		Matt, sand-blasted die, patterns		- -	- -	/£800
		Cupro-nickel				38 mm
1951	1,983,540	Festival of Britain Prooflike			£2	£4/£6
1951		In box of issue, green or purple			£4	£6/£8
1951		Proofs from the sets (same striking as previous)				£4/£6
1951		★ Patterns (or special proofs) (K.B.Coins 1990)				FDC £450
1951		Proofs, error strike on unedged blanks				£150/£250
1951		Matt, sand-blasted die, patterns		- -	- -	/£800

★ Not to be confused with 'prooflike' issue; the 'specials' have finer edge lettering and are, usually, accompanied by written provenance.

CROWNS

CUPRO-NICKEL 38mm

Date	Mintage		Fine	V.F.	E.F.	Abt. Unc/FDC.
ELIZABETH II						
1953	5,962,621	Equestrian	--	£1	£2	£4/£5
1953	Edge: FAITH AND TRUST I WILL BEAR UNTO YO (no 'U'):			£20	£30	£40/£50
1953	40,000	Proofs from sets and Maundy			£10	£20/£30
1953 ★	(K.B.Coins '94)	(Special proofs)			--	FDC £395
1953	Pattern	All-over frosting, dismal/matt				£600/£700
1953	Large date	Large emblems on cross			--	£350
1960	1,024,038	British Trades Fair		£1	£2	£4/£5
1960	70,000	Polished die specials			£4	£9/£16
1960 ★	(K.B.Coins '94)	(V.I.P. Proof)				FDC £475
1965	19,640,000	Churchill	---	---	30p	60p/ £1
1965	(K.B.Coins 1990)	Satin finish "special"				FDC £560

★ Frosted detail, highly polished field; not to be confused with 'ordinary' polished die proofs: the 'specials' have finer edge lettering and, usually, would be accompanied by written provenance.

DECIMAL CROWNS (Twentyfive Pence)

Date	Mintage		Proof from Selected Unc/Sets	.925 SILVER PROOF :		F.D.C. from/to
1972	7,452,100	Silver Wedding	£1/£6	1972	100,000	£18/£25
1977	36,989,000	Silver Jubilee	£1/£4	1977	377,000	£15/£20
1977	Selected coin in R.M. folder		£3/--			
	Queen Mother's 80th Birthday:					
1980	9,477,513		£1/£2	1980	83,672	£20/£30
1980	Selected coin in R.M. folder		£3/--			
1981	27,360,279	Royal Wedding	£1/£2	1981	218,142	£20/£30
1981	Selected coin in R.M. folder		£3/--			

1989 FOUR-CROWN-COLLECTION of the four silver proofs £125
(The Case, Booklet and Certificate should be preserved)

Smith's Private Pattern Decimals

1, 2, 5 and 10 cents	inverted reverse	£900
1, 2, 5 and 10 cents restrikes	upright reverse	£300

VICTORIA

DECIMAL 'FARTHING' of 1854 1/1000 of £1 a MILLE
1854 (noted 1994) "As struck" MODEL MILLE, GOTHIC HEAD, £125
1854 (noted 1996) "abtVF" £89 "gdVF" £99 - - - -

VICTORIA PATTERNS of 1857 BRITANNIA Reverse BRONZE

	Legend above Britannia:	Legend below Britannia:	
A)	ONE CENT	MDCCCLVII	16.5mm
B)	HALF FARTHING	ONE CENTIME	17.0mm
C)	TWO CENTS	MDCCCLVII	22.0mm
D)	ONE FARTHING	TWO CENTIMES	22.0mm
E)	FIVE CENTS	MDCCCLVII	27.0mm
F)	DECIMAL HALFPENNY	5 CENTIMES	27.5mm
G)	DECIMAL HALFPENNY	MDCCCLVII	27.0mm
H)	FIVE FARTHINGS	10 CENTIMES	33.5mm
H)	(Noted 1989 about V.F.)	FIVE FARTHINGS	£125
I)	DECIMAL PENNY	ONE TENTH OF A SHILLING	32.5mm
J)	TEN CENTS	ONE TENTH OF A SHILLING	32.5mm

VICTORIA PATTERNS of 1859 DATE BELOW HEAD BRONZE

K)	HALF DECIMAL PENNY	in wreath oak leaves/acorns	27mm
L)	HALF DECIMAL PENNY	ONE TWENTIETH SHILLING	27mm
M)	ONE DECIMAL PENNY	in wreath oak leaves/acorns	32mm
M)	(Noted 1986 E.F.)	Cupro-nickel and tin	£400
N)	ONE TENTH OF DECIMAL PENNY	A SHILLING	32mm
O)	⋆ DECIMAL PENNY ⋆	ONE TENTH OF A SHILLING	32mm
O2)	Has larger lettering and date between ornaments		32mm
O2)	(Noted 1986 E.F.)	Nickel-bronze	£250
P)	ONE DECIMAL PENNY	wreath laurel leaves/berries	32mm
Q)	As P)	but wreath half palm leaves, half oak leaves	32mm
R)	ONE DECIMAL PENNY	lion, shield, flags, bee-hive	32mm
S)	DECIMAL PENNY	crown, trident, laurel/oak wreath	32mm

See trident of 1961 2 CENTS

VICTORIA PATTERNS of 1859 SIZE REDUCED BRONZE

T)	DECIMAL HALF PENNY	laurel wreath with berries
U)	DECIMAL HALF PENNY	half laurel, half oak, crown
V)	DECIMAL HALF PENNY	complete circle of palm leaves
W)	ONE DECIMAL PENNY in exergue	lion and palm tree
X)	DECIMAL 1 PENNY	below large trident with dolphins
Y)	ONE PENNY Una and the Lion	DECIMAL in exergue
Z)	ONE DECIMAL PENNY	wreath alternating oak & laurel
Z2)	ONE DECIMAL PENNY	wreath half oak, half laurel
Z3)	Circle of roses, shamrocks, thistles around	ONE DECIMAL PENNY

First three 19.5 mm; W) to Z3) 27 mm.

Coins without date, or without denomination, not listed.

VICTORIA *Silver Patterns 1848 ONE TENTH OF A POUND 27 mm*

1)	Trident, wreath of oak leaves, 100 MILLES	-	ONE DECADE
2)	Trident, wreath of oak leaves, 100 MILLES	-	ONE CENTUM
3)	Trident - wreath of oak leaves	-	ONE FLORIN
4)	Royal cypher VR - emblems intertwined	-	ONE DECADE
4)	(noted 1988) ONE DECADE "as struck"		£725
5)	Royal cypher VR - emblems intertwined	-	ONE CENTUM
5)	(Spink 1988) ONE CENTUM "gdEF"		£695
6)	Royal cypher VR - emblems intertwined	-	ONE FLORIN
7)	Cruciform shields - rose at centre, below	-	ONE DIME
	Each of the seven with three different obverses (!)		
8)	Cruciform shields - laureate head	-	date below
9)	Cruciform shields - plain hair binding	-	date below
10)	1848 Cruciform shields - crowned bust	-	Godless florin
11)	1851 As 1848 but in Gothic style:		the date as mdcccli

Values for GODLESS and GOTHIC florins on page 33

ELIZABETH II *Decimal Patterns*

1 CENT - 1961 - ER - ONE DECIMAL PENNY - Bronze 20mm
2 CENTS - crown, ornamented trident - 1961 - Bronze 25mm
(1986 set of 1961 comprising 1, 2, 5, 10, 20 and 50 cents sold at Sotheby's for £2,400 plus buyers premium and VAT)

Aluminium quarter penny	Tudor Rose over 1/4	20mm
Bronze half penny	Welsh Dragon over 1/2	17mm
Bronze penny	Scottish Lion, St Andrews Cross	20mm
Bronze two pence	Britannia over large 2	26mm
Cupro-nickel five pence	Three Crowns over 5	23mm
Cupro-nickel ten pence	St George and The Dragon	28mm
Cupro-nickel twenty pence	Gartered Royal Arms	36mm

(in 1982, a decimal pattern for 20p dated 1963 @ £1,500)
(in 1986, full set of decimal patterns dated 1963 @ £4,500)
(in 1986, uniface set artist's copies at Spink's @ £900)

IN 1982 THE WORD 'NEW' WAS DISCONTINUED

Half New Penny

BRONZE 17mm — THE ROYAL CROWN

	Selected	Unc/Proof		Selected Unc/Proof			Selected Unc/Proof
1971	1,394,188,250	15p/£2	1976	50p/£2	1982		15p/£2
1971	Double headed	£200	1977	20p/£2	1983	7,600,000	25p/£2
1972	Proof ex-set	---/£3	1978	25p/£2	1984	158,820	£1/£2
1973	365,680,000	50p/£2	1979	20p/£2			
1974	365,448,000	50p/£2	1980	30p/£2			
1975	197,600,000	50p/£2	1981	60p/£2		Demonetized 31/12/84	

One New Penny

BRONZE 20mm to 1991 — Plated Steel 1992

A PORTCULLIS WITH CHAINS ROYALLY CROWNED

	Selected	Unc/Proof		Selected Unc/Proof		Selected Unc/Proof
1971	1,521,666,250	15p/£2	1981	60p/£2	1991	10p/£2
1972	Proof from set	---/£4	1982	40p/£2		
1973	280,196,000	50p/£2	1983	50p/£2	Now "magnetic"	
1974	330,892,000	60p/£2	1984	£1/£3	1992	£2/£2
1975	221,604,000	60p/£2	1985	20p/£2	1993	10p/£2
1976	241,800,000	50p/£2	1986	25p/£2	1994	10p/£2
1977	285,430,000	10p/£2	1987	10p/£2	1995	10p/£2
1978	292,770,000	£1/£2	1988	15p/£2	1996	10p/£2
1979	459,000,000	10p/£2	1989	10p/£2	1997	....
1980	416,304,000	10p/£2	1990	10p/£2	1998	....

Two New Pence

BRONZE 26mm to 1991 — Plated Steel 1992

THE BADGE OF THE PRINCE OF WALES

	Selected	Unc/Proof		Selected Unc/Proof		Selected Unc/Proof
1971	1,454,856,250	15p/£2	1982	£4/£2	1991	15p/£2
1972, 1973, 1974		---/£4	1983	£3/£2		
1975	145,545,000	75p/£2	1983	★ with old rev.	Now "magnetic"	
1976	181,379,000	75p/£2	1984	£1/£2	1992	15p/£2
1977	109,261,000	25p/£2	1985	20p/£2	1993	10p/£2
1978	189,658,000	£1/£3	1986	20p/£2	1994	10p/£2
1979	260,200,000	30p/£2	1987	20p/£2	1995	10p/£2
1980	408,527,000	25p/£2	1988	20p/£2	1996	10p/£2
1981	353,191,000	30p/£2	1989	20p/£2	1997	....
1981	Double "tail"	£100	1990	15p/£2	1998	....

1983 ★ two authenticated examples, so far, still inscribed 'NEW'.

1985 New MAKLOUF PORTRAIT of The Queen (see page 25)

1992 The twopence became "magnetic" being copper-plated steel.

Five Pence

CUPRO-NICKEL — 23mm 1968-1990 · 18mm 1990 onwards — A THISTLE ROYALLY CROWNED

	Selected	Unc/Proof		Selected Unc/Proof		Selected Unc/Proof
1968	98,868,250	50p/--	1982	£3/£4	1990 20,000 silver Piedfort	£28.95
1969	119,270,000	75p/--	1983	£3/£4		
1970	225,948,525	75p/--	1984	£2/£4	1991	20p/£2
1971	81,783,475	75p/£2	1985 from sets	£1/£2	1992	20p/£2
1972, 1973, 1974		---/£4	1986 from sets	£1/£2	1993	...........50p/£3
1975	86,550,000	50p/£2	1987	50p/£2	1994	50p/£2
1976	Proof from set	---/£4	1988	50p/£2	1995	---/£1
1977	24,308,000	35p/£2	1989	40p/£2	1996	---/£1
1978	61,000,000	50p/£3	1990 from sets	£3/£4	1997	....
1979	155,456,000	40p/£3	1990 18mm	20p/£2	1998	....
1980	220,566,000	30p/£2	1990 35,000 both sizes			
1981	Proof from set	---/£4	pairs in silver	£24.50		

Ten Pence

CUPRO-NICKEL — 28.5mm 1968-1990 · 24.5mm 1990 onwards — A LION PASSANT GUARDANT ROYALLY CROWNED

	Selected	Unc/Proof		Selected Unc/Proof		Selected Unc/Proof
1968	336,143,250	60p/--	1979	£1/£3	1990	£2/£5
1969	314,008,000	60p/--	1980	£1/£3	1991	£3/£5
1970	133,571,000	£2/--	1981	£1/£3	1992	£1/£3
1971	63,205,000	£2/£3	1982	£3/£5	1992 24.5mm	50p/£2
1972	Proof from set	---/£5	1983	£2/£4	1992 Silver Proof 'pair'	
1973	152,174,000	£1/£3	1984	£1/£3	of both sizes	£29.95
1974	92,741,000	£2/£4	1985 from sets	£1/£3	1993	50p/£2
1975	181,559,000	£1/£3	1986 from sets	£1/£3	1994	50p/£2
1976	228,220,000	£1/£3	1987 from sets	£1/£3	1995	50p/£1
1977	59,323,000	£1/£3	1988 from sets	£1/£3	1996	50p/£1
1978	Proof from sets	---/£4	1989 from sets	£1/£3	1997	....

The florin/two shilling/28.5mm tenpence piece was demonetized 30/6/93.

TWENTY PENCE

A DOUBLE ROSE ROYALLY CROWNED

CUPRO-NICKEL 21.4mm

		Selected Unc/Proof		Selected Unc/Proof
1982	740,815,000	50p/£6	1990	50p/£5
1982	25,000 silver Piedfort	--/£40	1991	50p/£5
1983	158,463,000	50p/£5	1992	40p/£4
1984	65,350,965	75p/£5	1993	40p/£3
1985	74,273,699	50p/£5	1993 *	1 known, so far, struck in steel
1986	From the sets	£1/£5	1994	40p/£2
1987	137,450,000	75p/£5	1995	30p/£1
1988	38,038,344	45p/£4	1996	....
1989	109,128,890	45p/£4	1997	....

* R. Colliass Esq reports, and the Royal Mint confirms, a steel blank intended for a 1p struck in error with the dies of the 1993 20p (source 1995)

FIFTY PENCE

CUPRO-NICKEL 30 mm

Proofs, are those taken from the sets unless otherwise indicated.

		Selected Unc/Proof		Sel.Unc/Proof		Sel.Unc/Proof
1969	188,400,000	£2/£4	1981	£2/£4	1991	£3/£6
1969	Double "head"	£150	1981 Double "tail"	£200	1992	/£5
1970	19,461,000	£2/£4			1992/93	** /£5
1971 & 73	from sets	--/£4	1982	£2/£5	** Silver	£24
1973	* 89,775,000	£2/--	1983	£2/£5	** Piedfort	£45
Proofs *	356,616 cased	£4	1984	£2/£5	** Gold	£375
1974 & 75	from sets	--/£4	1985	£2/£5	1994 ex-sets	£3/£6
1976	43,746,500	£2/£4	1986	£2/£5	1995 ex-sets	£3/£6
1977	49,536,000	£2/£4	1987	£2/£5	1996 ex-sets	£3/£6
1978	72,005,500	£2/£4	1988	£3/£5	1997 ***	
1979	58,680,000	£2/£4	1989	£3/£5		
1980		£2/£4	1990	£3/£6		

* EEC Commemoratives (also a few V.I.P piedforts)

** New design to commemmorate Britain's Presidency/Council of Ministers

1994 "D-Day" in folder £2 · Silver Proof £24 · Piedfort £45 · Gold £375

*** "Coin News" June 1996 reporting on the new, smaller (27.5mm) 50p dated 1997, states that Richard Lobel (Coincraft) was able to purchase 10 of them in the Netherlands!

DECIMAL COINAGE ONE POUND (One Hundred Pence)

Pale-yellow mixture of metals · 22.5 mm dia. · 3.1 mm thick has grained (milled) edge, with incuse (struck in) lettering.
England and Northern Ireland variants read: DECUS ET TUTAMEN (An Ornament and a Safeguard) first used to prevent the "clipping" of coins

Scotland: NEMO ME IMPUNE LACESSIT (No One Provokes Me with Impunity)

For Wales: PLEIDOL WYF I'M GWALD (True Am I to My Country)

Date	Mintage		Unc./Proof
1983	434,000,000	Royal Coat of Arms general issue	£3/£5
1983	484,900	Selected general issue in wallet	£4/- -
1983	50,000	Sterling silver (.925) proofs	£25
1983	10,000	Silver Piedfort proofs.	£145
1984	110,000,000	Thistle for Scotland general issue	£2/£4
1984	27,960	Selected general issue in wallet	£5/- -
1984	44,855	Sterling silver (.925) proofs	£25
1984	15,000	Silver Piedfort proofs.	£55
1985	178,000,000	Leek for Wales general issue	£3/£5
1985		Selected general issue in wallet	£4/- -
1985	50,000	Sterling silver (.925) proofs	£25
1985	15,000	Silver Piedfort proofs.	£55

Date	Mintage		Unc.	Proofs from Sets ↓
1986	Not revealed	Flax Plant for Northern Ireland	£2	£5
		Selected general issue in wallet	£4	
1986	50,000	Sterling silver (.925) proofs	£25	
1986	15,000	Silver Piedfort proofs.	£50	
1987		An Oak Tree for general issue	£2	£5
		Selected general issue in wallet	£4	
1987	50,000	Sterling silver (.925) proofs	£25	
1987	15,000	Silver Piedfort proofs.	£50	
1988		The Royal Arms of H.M. The Queen (Derek Gorringe)	£2	£4
		Selected general issue in wallet	£3	
1988	50,000	Sterling silver (.925) proofs	£25	
1988	15,000	Silver Piedfort proofs.	£50	
1989		Re-appearance of the Thistle Pound	£2	£4
1989	25,000	Sterling silver (.925) proofs	£25	
1989	10,000	Silver Piedfort proofs.	£60	
1990		Re-appearance of the Leek Pound	£2	£4
1990	25,000	Sterling silver (.925) proofs	£25	
1991		Re-appearance of the Flax Pound	£2	£4
1991	25,000	Sterling silver (.925) proofs	£25	
1992		General Issue (Oak Tree)	£2	£4
1992	25,000	Sterling silver (.925) proofs	£25	
1993		General Issue · Royal Arms	£2	£4
1993	25,000	Sterling silver (.925) proofs	£25	
1993	12,500	Silver Peidfort proofs	£50	

Date	Mintage		Selected Unc.	Proof
1994		First of New Series		
		Scottish Lion Rampant	£2	£5
1994	25,000	Sterling silver (.925) proofs	£25	- - -
1994	12,500	Silver Piedfort proofs	£50	
1994		Presentation folder, nickel-brass	£3	
1995		Welsh Dragon · nickel-brass:	£2	£4
		Presentation folder · English text	£4	
		Presentation folder · text in Welsh	£5	
1995	25,000	Sterling silver (.925) proofs	£25	
1995	12,500	Silver Piedfort proofs	£50	
1996		N. Ireland Celtic Cross	£2	£4
1996		Presentation folder, nickel-brass	£4	
1996	25,000	Sterling silver (.925) proofs	£25	
1996	12,500	Silver Piedfort proofs	£50	
1997		....		

Issue Price or Uncirc. Values

TWO POUNDS

28.4 mm

1986 COMMEMORATING EDINBURGH COMMONWEALTH GAMES

Thistle, Wreath, Cross of St.Andrew		£3	Selected in wallet	£6
125,000	Nickel-brass proofs	£5	125,000 .500 silver	£15
75,000	925 silver proofs	£25	15,000 gold proofs	£280

1989 COMMEMORATING 300th ANNIVERSARY BILL OF RIGHTS

William & Mary. Not for general issue, but still legal tender.

Bill of Rights	£3	Selected in wallet	£5
Claim of Right	£4	Selected in wallet	£6

Pair, as picture, selected, in Official blister-pack £10
25,000 each Bill and Claim proofs in silver singles £24
10,000 pairs Bill AND Claim proofs, silver, piedfort, pairs £80

1994 COMMEMORATING TERCENTENARY of THE BANK OF ENGLAND

Edge: SIC VOS NON VOBIS (Thus you labour but not for yourselves)
Uncirculated £3 · Blister-pack £3.95 · Proofs from sets £6
Silver proof, 40,000, £25 · Silver Proof Piedfort £50
Gold 'TWO POUNDS' £325 · error not showing value £425

1995 WORLD WAR II · DOVE OF PEACE · edge: IN PEACE GOODWILL

Blister-pack £3.95 · Silver proof, 40,000, £24.50 · Gold £350

1995 UNITED NATIONS 50th ANNIVERSARY · 1945 - 1995

Unciculated £3 · Folder £5 · Silver Proof, 100,000, £27
Silver Proof Piedfort, 10,000, £50 · Gold Proof, 17,500, £300

1996 EUROPEAN FOOTBALL CHAMPIONSHIP

Uncirculated £3 · Folder £5 · Silver Proof, 50,000, £27
Silver Proof Piedfort 10,000, £50 · Gold, 2,750, £350
Missing designer's initials (like old-time laces) £6

38.61mm

FIVE POUNDS

1990 COMMEMORATING THE QUEEN MOTHER's 90th BIRTHDAY

Interlaced Es - Rose and Thistle - Legal Tender £5
Pack £10 · Silver Proofs, 150,000, £30 · Gold Proofs, 2,500, £700

1993 THE CORONATION ANNIVERSARY 1953/1993

Queen's 1953 portrait encircled by mounted trumpeters/swords/sceptres
Pack £10 · Silver Proofs, 100,000, £30 · Gold Proofs, 2,500, £625

1996 COMMEMORATING H.M. THE QUEEN'S 70th BIRTHDAY

Pack £10 · Silver Proofs, 70,000, £30 · Gold Proofs, 2,750, £650

PROOF and Uncirculated SETS

★ = plus Royal Mint medallion

GEORGE IV

			F.D.C. from / to
1826	140 sets (11)	Farthing to five pounds	£17,000/£20,000

WILLIAM IV

				F.D.C. from / to
1831	145 sets (14)	Maundy replaces £5		£12,500/£18,000
	Silver only (8)	(Spink 1988)	E.F. £4,400	------

VICTORIA

				F.D.C. from / to
1839	300 sets (15)	in spade shaped case which includes: the Una-and-The-Lion gold £5		£25,000/£28,000
1853	460 (16)	Quarter-farthing to Gothic 5/-		£20,000/£25,000
1887	797 sets (11)	unofficial cases	3d to £5	£4,500/ £6,000
1887	287 sets		3d to 5/-	£750/ £950
1893	773 sets (10)	rarely intact	3d to £5	£4,500/ £6,500
1893	Short set of six silver coins		3d to 5/-	£900/ £1,200

EDWARD VII

			F.D.C. from / to
1902	8,066 sets (13)	Maundy 1d to £5 (matt)	£1,000/ £1,500
1902	7,057 sets (11)	Maundy 1d to sovereign	£400/ £550

GEORGE V

			F.D.C. from / to
1911	2,812 sets (12)	Maundy 1d to £5	£2,000 £2,500
1911	952 sets (10)	Maundy 1d to sovereign	£600/ £750
1911	2,241 sets (8)	Maundy penny to half-crown	£200/ £325
1927	15,030 sets (6)	3d to crown	£185/ £250

GEORGE VI

			F.D.C. from / to
1937	5,501 sets (4)	Half-sovereign to £5	£1,500/£1,800
1937	26,402 sets (15)	Farthing to crown + Maundy	£90/ £120
1950	17,513 sets (9)	Farthing to half-crown	£35/ £50
1951	20,000 sets (10)	Farthing to crown	£50/ £75

ELIZABETH II

			F.D.C. from / to
1953	40,000 sets (10)	Farthing to crown (5/-)	£30/ £42
1953	*	A large number of sets in plastic wallet (9)	£9/ £12
1968	*	Decimal souvenir sets, mixed dates in folder	£1/ £3
1970	750,000	Last Sterling $1/2$d to 2/6d + medallion	£10/ £15

* non-proof, selected currency coins

1953 "plastic" sets sometimes (rarely) found with 1/4d Obverse 1 Rev. B and must, therefore, be at least as rare as that coin (see page 6)

				F.D.C. from / to
1971	350,000	(6) ★	half to 50p	£10/£12
1972	150,000	(7) ★	plus Crown	£10/£12
1973	100,000	(6) ★	half to EEC 50p	£7/ £9
1974	100,000	(6) ★	half to 50p	£6/£10
1975	100,000	(6) ★	half to 50p	£7/ £9
1976	100,000	(6) ★	half to 50p	£7/ £9
1977	193,000	(7) ★	Jubilee Crown	£10/£14
1978	88,100	(6) ★	half to 50p	£12/£16
1979	81,000	(6) ★	half to 50p	£12/£18
1980	10,000	(4)	half-sov to £5	£850
1980	143,400	(6) ★	half to 50p	£5/£10
1981	5,000	(9)	½p to gold £5	£600
1981	2,500	(2)	crown & sov.	£90/£140
1981	100,300	(6) ★	half to 50p	£5/£10
1982	2,500	(4)	half-sov to £5	£800
1982	106,800	(7) ★	plus new 20p	£5/£10
1982	205,000	(7)	Uncirc in folder	£3/ £5
1983	12,500	(3)	½ sov, sov, £2	£300
1983	107,800	(8) ★	plus 20p & £1	£8/£14
1983	637,100	(8)	Uncirc in folder	£5/ £6
1984	7,095	(3)	½ sov, sov, £5	£600
1984	125,000	(8) ★	Scottish £1	£8/£14
1984	158,820	(8)	Uncirc in folder	£5/ £6

				ISSUE PRICE
1985	125,000	(7) ★	1p to Welsh £1 Maklouf portrait, blue leatherette case	£18.75
			de-luxe red leather case	£25.75
1985		(7)	Uncirc in folder	£4.75
1986	125,000	(8) ★	N.I. £1 & C/wealth £2, in blue leatherette case	£21.25
			in de-luxe red leather case	£28.25
1986		(8)	Uncirc in folder	£7.95
1987	125,000	(7) ★	1p to English Oak £1 in blue leatherette case	£18.95
			in de-luxe red leather case	£25.95
1987		(7)	Uncirc in folder	£5.25
1988	125,000	(7) ★	1p to Royal Arms £1 in blue leatherette case	£18.95
			in de-luxe red leather case	£25.95
1988		(7)	Uncirc in folder	£5.25
1989	125,000	(8) ★	1p to 'Orange' £2 x 2 in blue leatherette case	£22.95
			in de-luxe red leather case	£29.95
1989		(8)	Uncirc in folder	£5.75
1989			Boy/Girl Baby Packs in Blue/Pink either @	£9.95
1990	100,000	(8) ★	1p, (both 5p), 50p to Welsh £1: in blue leatherette case	£21.95
			in de-luxe red leather case	£28.95
1990		(8)	Uncirc in folder	£6.25
1990			Boy/Girl Baby Packs in Blue/Pink either @	£9.95
1991	100,000	(7) ★	1p, to N.I. £1 in blue leatherette case	£23.50
			in de-luxe red leather case	£30.60
1991		(8)	Uncirc in folder	£7.10
1991			Baby Packs	£11.20
1991			L.s.d. set (dated 1967)	£14.25
1992	100,000	(9) ★	1p, (10p x 2), (50p x 2) to £1 in blue leatherette case	£27.50
			in de-luxe red leather case	£34.50
1992		(9)	uncirc in folder	£8.75
1992			Baby Packs	£13.95
1992			Wedding Pack	£13.95
1993	100,000	(8) ★	1p to £5	
1993			in blue leatherette case	£28.75
			in de-luxe red leather case	£35.50
1993		(8)	uncirc 1p to £1 (50p x 2)	£8.75
1993			Baby Gift Set	£13.95
1993			Wedding Collection	£16.50
1994	100,000	(8) ★	1p to £1	
1994			in blue leatherette case	£24.75
			in de-luxe red leather case	£32.50
1994		(8)	uncirc in folder	£8.75
1994			Baby Gift Set	£13.95
1994			Wedding Collection	£14.95
1995	100,000	(8) ★	1p to £1	
1995			in blue leatherette case	£24.75
			in de-luxe red leather case	£32.50
1995		(8)	uncirc in folder	£8.75
1995			Baby Gift Set	£13.95
1995			Wedding Collection	£14.95
1996	100,000	(9) ★	1p to £5 in blue leatherette case	£29.75
			in de-luxe red leather case	£37.50
1996		(8)	1p to £1 in folder	£9.50
1996			Baby Gift Set	£14.95
1996			Wedding Collection	£14.95
1996			LSD mixed/Decimal 1996 set	£25.00
1997			....	

GEORGE III (Page 1 refers)

The George III pamphlet, referred to in the 23rd edition, grew into a 16 page booklet and proved very popular. This is still available, updated of course, @ £1 post free.

The booklet (and pamphlet), regardless of condition will be able to be used against the purchase price of the comprehensive George III now in preparation. Purchasers of the book/pamphlet will be informed as soon as the new George III (to include George III gold) is available.

37·4